Tolstoy

THE PROFILES IN LITERATURE SERIES

GENERAL EDITOR: B. C. SOUTHAM, M.A., B.LITT. (OXON.)
*Formerly Department of English, Westfield College,
University of London*

Tolstoy

by Ronald Hayman

LONDON

ROUTLEDGE & KEGAN PAUL
NEW YORK: HUMANITIES PRESS

First published 1970
by Routledge & Kegan Paul Ltd
Broadway House, 68-74 Carter Lane
London, E.C.4
Printed in Great Britain
by Northumberland Press Ltd
Gateshead
© Ronald Hayman 1970
ISBN 0 7100 6694 5 (c)
ISBN 0 7100 6695 3 (p)

The Profiles in Literature Series

This series is designed to provide the student of literature and the general reader with a brief and helpful introduction to the major novelists and prose writers in English, American and foreign literature.

Each volume will provide an account of an individual author's writing career and works, through a series of carefully chosen extracts illustrating the major aspects of the author's art. These extracts are accompanied by commentary and analysis, drawing attention to particular features of the style and treatment. There is no pretence, of course, that a study of extracts can give a sense of the works as a whole, but this selective approach enables the reader to focus his attention upon specific features, and to be informed in his approach by experienced critics and scholars who are contributing to the series.

The volumes will provide a particularly helpful and practical form of introduction to writers whose works are extensive or which present special problems for the modern reader, who can then proceed with a sense of his bearings and an informed eye for the writer's art.

An important feature of these books is the extensive reference list of the author's works and the descriptive list of the most useful biographies, commentaries and critical studies.

B.C.S.

Acknowledgments

The author and publisher wish to thank the following for permission to use copyright material:

Penguin Books Ltd.

Hamish Hamilton Ltd.

Oxford University Press

Contents

CONTENTS

viii

Biographical outline

At the end of the year he was sent to St. Petersburg as a courier.

1856 Promoted to the rank of lieutenant for bravery at the Battle of the Chernaya. Requested eleven months furlough and returned to Yasnaya Polyana. A long flirtation with Valerya Arsenyev led not to marriage but to the short story *Family Happiness* (1858-9).

1862 Married Sonya Behrs; finished *The Cossacks*.

1863- Worked on *War and Peace*.
1869

1873- Worked on *Anna Karenina*.
1877

1878 Worked on another historical novel (about the Decembrist uprising).

1879 Abandoned it, intending to devote his life to religion. Wrote *A Confession*.

1874- A series of religious works, including *Critique of*
1884 *Dogmatic Theology, The Four Gospels Harmonised and Translated* and *What I Believe* and simple morality tales like *What Men Live By* intended for uneducated people.

1886 Wrote *The Death of Ivan Ilyich* and *The Devil*.

1888- Wrote *The Kreutzer Sonata*.
1889

1889 Started 'Koni's Story' (later *Resurrection*) but put it aside.

1895 First draft of *Resurrection*. Started *Master and Man*.

1898 Wrote *What is Art?*

1899 Finished *Resurrection*.

1901- Worked on *Hadji Murad*.
1904

1910 Died.

Tolstoy: his life and works

Introduction

'No English novelist,' E. M. Forster declared in *Aspects of the Novel*, 'is as great as Tolstoy—that is to say has given so complete a picture of man's life, both on its domestic and heroic side.' An attempt to explain in one short sentence what it is that makes Tolstoy so great is an attempt at the impossible. So, of course, is an attempt to explain it in one short book, which cannot be adequate to describe the massive achievement of Tolstoy's novels and stories. But perhaps that is not a good reason for not writing it.

War and Peace and *Anna Karenina* are unrivalled for the depth of their penetration into the reality of the characters and into the historical background. Unerringly, Tolstoy singles out the right details to tell us what matters about the way his people live. His narrative method works like a super-subtle camera lens which can narrow its focus to a close-up on private feelings and thoughts, then, an instant later, open out to a panorama of the social and political situations.

No novelist gives us a stronger feeling of getting to

know his characters. We see so many facets of them from as many different viewpoints as they interact with other characters, react to the pressure of historical events and develop with the passage of time. We watch them growing older almost in the same way that we watch our friends, and Tolstoy too watches them with love, a love which is all the greater for his clear-sighted awareness of their faults.

War and Peace is undoubtedly one of the greatest novels that have ever been written but Tolstoy did not think of it as a novel at all. He described *Anna Karenina* (which was written later) as his first novel; what concerned him primarily in *War and Peace* was historical truth. Though he was in his late thirties when he wrote it, he was fulfilling an ambition he had harboured since his early twenties. 'To write the genuine history of present-day Europe, that is an aim for the whole of one's life.' The book is made up of fact and fiction mixed as never before. Historical characters like Napoleon and Tsar Alexander rub shoulders with invented characters. The historical characters speak invented dialogue. The invented characters are put into solid historical situations. Fiction is yoked to the service of the truth.

In a sense, of course, every good novelist is writing fiction in order to tell the truth. There are few biographies and few journals which can give you as clear a picture as a novel can of what is going on at a certain place, at a certain time. Especially if the novelist picks his protagonists, as Tolstoy did, to be representative of different sections of society, their experiences will be a distillation of contemporary social history. High politics and humble domestic life all become part of the same picture. As we shall see, when E. M. Forster spoke of the *completeness* of Tolstoy's picture, he was using the right word.

His work

Tolstoy was more of an impressionist than a naturalist but he was above all a realist. Every novelist has to select, and selection implies simplification, but Tolstoy, even in his early stories, tried to avoid the falsification that results from focusing exclusively on one characteristic. 'In the course of my life,' he wrote in a draft of his first story *Childhood*, 'I have never met a man who was all bad, all pride, all good or all intelligence. In modesty I can always find a repressed urge towards pride, I see stupidity in the most intelligent book, intelligent things in the conversation of the greatest fool alive, etc.' This sensitivity to the co-presence of opposites is one of the qualities that enabled him to see both emotions and physical realities for what they actually were. He was impatient with the affectations of conventional literary metaphor because they distorted reality. 'I never saw lips of coral, but I have seen them the colour of brick; nor turquoise eyes, but I have seen them the colour of laundry blueing'.

On the first page of *Childhood*, he describes how an emotion changes, within minutes, into its opposite. When the ten-year-old hero is woken up at seven in the morning by his clumsy German tutor, who swats a fly so that it falls dead on his face, the boy's irritation borders on hatred; but when the man starts tickling his heels to wake him up, he can't help saying to himself, 'How nice he is, and how fond of us! How could I have had such horrid thoughts about him just now?' Later on in the story we get an emotional reversal which also involves a reversal of intention. The boy's father has intended to sack the tutor but when the warm-hearted German comes into his study, intending to put all his grievances about the family's ingratitude into one angry speech, he finds himself bursting into tears and offering to go on work-

3

ing without a salary. The father keeps him on.

Tolstoy's genius was immediately recognised by Russian critics as soon as *Childhood* appeared in a magazine in 1852. What made the story so outstanding was its freshness and uncluttered directness. It also showed what a good eye Tolstoy had for physical detail. The dryness of the old princess's hand, for instance, or the tufts of the boy's hair which stick up help to define our impression of them. But it was only later that Tolstoy developed his mastery in distilling inner significance out of his carefully selected details.

No detail must be neglected in art, for a button half-undone may explain a whole side of a person's character. It is absolutely essential to mention that button. But it has to be described in terms of the person's inner life, and attention must not be diverted from important things to focus on accessories and trivia.

During the ten years that he was working on *The Cossacks* (1852-62) he greatly refined his technique. His physical description of the old peasant Yeroshka (see Extract 1, p. 15) gives clear pointers both to the kind of life the old man leads and to what goes on inside him. Yeroshka served Tolstoy as a rough sketch for Platon Karatayev, the peasant who has such an important place in *War and Peace* (see Extract 2, p. 17). The description of Karatayev is more selective, and not only are the physical details directly relevant to the man's inner life but indirectly to the effect he has on the hero's inner development.

The reversals of emotion and intention in *War and Peace* also show how much Tolstoy's technique had developed—and his vision deepened—since *Childhood*. One of the most striking reversals comes when Prince Andrei sees the man he has most reason to be jealous of in the military hospital. Three hundred pages back we

4

had a detailed account of how the vain, handsome, un-scrupulous Anatole Kuragin won Natasha's love away from her fiancé, Andrei, and almost succeeded in elop-ing with her when her parents were away from the house. Now, in the hospital, Andrei does not at first recognise Anatole in a miserable, sobbing, shattered creature who has just had his leg amputated. It would be easy to sen-timentalise the love and pity Andrei feels for the man he thought he hated, but by making his mind go back to his first memory of seeing Natasha at a ball, Tolstoy finds the right bridge to the new emotion.

In the early work, though there were switches of emotion and subtle contrasts and variations in almost every scene, the inter-relationship between the scenes was not as carefully structured as in *War and Peace*, *Anna Karenina* and *Resurrection*. They are all built around a polarity between opposites, and the chiaroscuro in each part contributes to the composition of the whole. The basic motive of *War and Peace* was to contrast the reality of history as people experienced it with the unreal pic-ture presented by the historians. His method, as Isaiah Berlin has put it,[1] involved juxtaposing reality with the distorting medium. It also involved juxtaposing a series of scenes representative of the personal relationships between individuals living out their private lives with scenes representative of the public events which changed both their living conditions and their inner development.

The two heroes, Andrei and Pierre, both stand out from the background of society life because their values quarrel with those which are commonly accepted. They also contrast with each other. When they argue over a dinner table, they seem to have followed opposite courses in relation to altruism. Pierre says that he almost ruined his life by living for himself and only found happiness when he started trying to live for others. Andrei replies

[1] Isaiah Berlin, *The Hedgehog and the Fox*.

5

that after living for honour and glory, he has found more peace by living for himself. Andrei is sceptical, elegant, ambitious and an atheist up to his deathbed change of heart; Pierre is credulous, gauche and symbolically short-sighted. He plans to assassinate Napoleon with the same naïve impulsiveness that earlier made him plunge into Freemasonry and it is typical of him that the escapade ends with his saving the life of a child.

In *Anna Karenina*, the adulterous lovers, Anna and Vronsky, and the couple who marry, Levin and Kitty, are contrasted rather as the two heroes are contrasted in *War and Peace*, while the plot weaves its complex way between its two poles. Both novels introduce a vast array of subordinate themes and for a writer who has been accused (by Henry James for instance) of indifference to form, Tolstoy succeeds remarkably well in imposing unity on his massive and diverse material in both novels.

But of the two *Anna Karenina* comes closer to complete success. The inter-relationship between the parts is subtler and more satisfying. History, as such, is no longer a factor in Tolstoy's complex calculus of events and personal relationships accordingly bulk larger, with the result that Tolstoy's own voice is less obtrusive in the narrative. His attitudes merge more fully into those of his characters. He rewrote the scene between Levin and the priest (Part Five, Section 1) four times to make sure of not betraying his own sympathies.

In *War and Peace* he was anxious to prove that the individual's willpower and his mental or physical condition had only a superficial influence on the course of events. This forced him into some very explicit arguments about causation—as in refuting the contention that the French army would have done better at the Battle of Borodino if Napoleon hadn't had a cold in his head. In *Anna Karenina* Tolstoy did not try to theorise about what it was that made things happen, and this gave him greater

6

freedom in evolving the plot, which sometimes seemed to be out of his control. In a letter to the critic Strakhov, he said that he had not at first thought that Vronsky's attempted suicide was necessary. 'I had begun to revise my rough draft and suddenly, by some means that was totally unexpected but ineluctable, Vronsky determined to put a bullet through his head, and it later became clear that that scene was organically indispensable'.

There are many scenes in *Anna Karenina* where the effect rests largely on the co-presence of opposites or the sudden reversal of a feeling or intention. When Karenin is left alone in a room with the baby daughter his wife has born to Vronsky, looking into the baby's face makes Karenin's expression change from despondency to a smile and suddenly feeling 'vexed with his wife for not paying more attention to this sweet baby', he no longer wants to go in to see Anna in the bedroom.

This is a small and comic change of volition; the biggest and most tragic is Anna's at the moment of throwing herself under the train. Watching for the space between the wheels to draw level with her, she drops on her hands under the truck,

and with a light movement, as though she would rise again at once, sank on to her knees. At that same instant she became horror-struck at what she was doing. 'Where am I? What am I doing? Why?' She tried to get up, to throw herself back; but something huge and relentless struck her on the head and dragged her down on her back. 'God forgive me everything!' she murmured, feeling the impossibility of struggling. A little peasant muttering something was working at the rails. And the candle by which she had been reading the book filled with trouble and deceit, sorrow and evil, flared up with a brighter light, illuminating for her everything that before had been enshrouded in darkness, flickered, grew dim and went out for ever.

7

This is how Part Seven ends but there are another fifty pages before the book is over. Just as the narrative part of *War and Peace* (before the theoretical second part of the Epilogue) focuses finally on the family life of Pierre and Natasha with their children, *Anna Karenina* ends with Levin's beginning to feel real love towards his baby. It is only after a storm in which the child's life might have been in danger and after reproaching Kitty for not taking more care that Levin finds how deep his own feelings are.

In the three major stories, *The Death of Ivan Ilyich* (1886), *The Kreutzer Sonata* (1888-9) and *Master and Man* (1895) the moment of death (or killing) provides the main climax to which the whole action builds up. Like Levin's brother in *Anna Karenina*, who spoke, just before dying, 'as if all had become clear to him', Ivan Ilyich attains a higher level of awareness on his deathbed than ever before in his life. 'It was revealed to him that his life had not been what it ought to have been but that it was still possible to put it right.' With a sudden altruism, he starts to feel more sorry for his family than for himself. The pain that has plagued him vanishes and when he hears a nearby voice saying 'It is all over', 'he caught the words and repeated them in his soul. "Death is over," he said to himself. "It is no more." '

In *The Kreutzer Sonata*, the misogynist narrator realises that love and animosity are one and the same animal feeling, that the quarrels he has always had with his wife are integral to the mutual affection. Similarly, in the instant of killing her, he is aware of also not wanting to do what he is doing. 'Having plunged the dagger in I pulled it out immediately, trying to remedy what had been done and to stop it.' And in *Master and Man*, the best of these three stories, the master leaves his servant to freeze to death in the snow (see Extract 13, p. 55). The reversal of this intention is partly fortuitous: he gets lost

8

and has to follow the horse who leads him back to his abandoned sledge. But once there, he saves the man's life by lying on top of him in his fur coat. He freezes to death himself but in his last moment of consciousness he achieves a joyful altruism which makes his business preoccupations seem trivial and his own life seem to be present not in himself but in the peasant.

Altruism is also the force that activates Prince Nekhludov, the hero of *Resurrection*, once he has acknowledged the extent of his own involvement in the life of another human being. As a young man, he seduced Maslova, a servant girl, who became pregnant, lost her job and had to become a prostitute. When she is sentenced to four years hard labour for a crime she hasn't committed, he tries to save her, and, failing, follows her to Siberia, offering to marry her. As she sees it, his altruism is spurious: he is trying to use her, as he used her before, for his own ends—to atone. But the relationship, though it never leads to marriage, leads them both to a higher level of awareness.

The novel, like *War and Peace* and *Anna Karenina*, is bi-polar but this time one of the poles is set in the proletarian hemisphere, and the action gravitates more and more away from aristocratic reception rooms to squalid prisons and detention camps. Tolstoy was angry at the injustice of the system by which convicts, who were often innocent of the crimes for which they had been sentenced, were treated as if they were sub-human and, in effect, murdered when exposed to typhus infection and forced marches which were bound to kill at least some of them.

Admirable though Tolstoy's righteous indignation is, it makes him less sensitive than usual to the co-presence of opposite elements inside the individual. Perhaps it is an awareness of this lack in the novel that encourages him to formulate a doctrine of opposites, as if to remind himself:

We may say of a man that he is more frequently kind than cruel, wise than foolish, energetic than apathetic, or vice versa—but it could never be true to say of one man that he is kind or wise, and of another that he is wicked or foolish. Yet this is our method of classifying mankind, and a very false method it is. Men are like rivers. The water is alike in all of them; but every river is narrow in some places and wide in others; here swift and there sluggish, here clear and there turbid; cold in winter and warm in summer. The same may be said of men. Every man bears within himself the germs of every human quality, displaying all in turn; and a man can often seem unlike himself—yet he still remains the same man.

Resurrection, Book I, ch. xix.

Taken as a whole, Tolstoy's fiction probably does more than the work of any other novelist to demonstrate the truth of this statement.

Scheme of extracts

The extracts are grouped under two headings:

1. Narrative Method
2. Areas of Subject Matter

The first group is subdivided into six sections:

Characterisation
Group Scenes
Inner and Outer Landscape
Inner Monologue
Dialogue
Satire and Irony

In each section the extracts have been arranged chrono-
logically to illustrate the development of Tolstoy's technique and the commentary endeavours to give pointers to
this.

PART ONE

Narrative method

Characterisation

In his early work, like *The Cossacks*, Tolstoy tended to give a full physical description of a character on his first appearance, rather like a stage direction in the script of a play. Later he was more skilful in conveying information about one character through other characters' impressions of him, so that we get to know him gradually, as they do.

Yeroshka is the first important peasant in Tolstoy's work and this description comes when the hero Olenin, a cadet, first meets him.

I

It was plain by the old man's face that he liked the cadet; also he was quick to see that here was someone he could get free drinks from, and therefore he could afford to present him with a brace of pheasants.

A few moments later Gaffer Yeroshka's figure appeared in the doorway of the hut, and it was only then that Olenin realized the enormous size and sturdy build of the man, whose red-brown face with its bushy snow-white beard was all furrowed by heavy lines and wrinkles, the result of hard work and age. His legs, arms and shoulders displayed the fine muscular development of a young man. There were deep scars on his head under the short-cropped hair. His thick, sinewy neck was checkered with criss-cross folds, like the neck of a bull. His horny hands were bruised and scratched. He stepped lightly and easily over the threshold, divested himself of his gun which he stood in a corner, and casting a quick glance round the room shrewdly estimated the value of its contents; then with out-turned toes and treading softly in his rawhide sandals he came into the middle of the room, bringing with him a penetrating but not unpleasant smell compounded of wine, vodka, gunpowder and dried blood. He bowed towards the ikons, smoothed his beard, and then, approaching Olenin, held out a thick black hand.

'Koshkildy,' he said. 'That's "Good-day to you" in Tartar, or "Peace to you," as they say.'

'Koshkildy, I know,' answered Olenin, giving him his hand.

'Ah, but you don't know. You don't know the right order, you ignoramus!' said Yeroshka, shaking his head reproachfully. 'If anyone says "Koshkildy" to you, you must answer "Alla rasi bo sun"—"God save you". That's how it goes, brother, and not "Koshkildy". But I'll teach you all of that. We had a lad here, Ilya Moseich, one of your Russians, and he and me was bosom pals. A fine fellow he was—drunk, thief and hunter. Ah, what a hunter, by heaven! I taught him everything.'

'And what will you teach me?' asked Olenin, who was becoming more and more interested in the old man.

'I will take you out hunting, and learn you to fish. I will show you the Chechens, and if you wants to find a girl I will do that for you too. That's the sort I am! . . . A wag I am.' And the old man laughed. 'I'll sit me down. I'm tired. Karga?' he added inquiringly.

'And what does "Karga" mean?' asked Olenin.

'It means "All right" in Georgian. I'm always a-saying of it—it's a saying of mine, me favourite word: karga, karga, I sez it like that, and it means I'm not serious.

Now, what about the wine, brother? Ain't you a-sending out for some?'

The Cossacks, ch. xi.

Henri Troyat has pointed out the thematic resemblance of *The Cossacks* to Pushkin's *Gypsies* and Lermontov's *A Hero of Our Time*. Though Olenin is also trying to find a substitute for the artificialities of civilised society and trying to integrate himself into the life of a more primitive community, the story is more realistic and less romantic, based, like so much of Tolstoy's writing, fairly directly on personal experience. When he went to the Caucasus, Tolstoy, like Olenin, was a jaded aristocrat in his twenties, bored with his idle life of flirtations and gambling, but greedy for fun and primed to respond warmly to a character like this. Much of the dialogue suffers in the translation, as it always does with uneducated characters who speak a dialect, but Yeroshka's vitality comes through, together with a boyish mischievousness which, in a society like this, can more easily survive in an old man.

Platon Karatayev in *War and Peace* is much more subtly presented. Pierre meets him when he is taken prisoner by the French.

2

In the shed, where Pierre spent four weeks, there were twenty-three soldiers, three officers and two civilian functionaries, all prisoners like himself.

Pierre remembered them afterwards as misty figures, except Platon Karatayev, who for ever remained in his mind as a most vivid and precious memory, and the very personification of all that was Russian, warm-hearted and —'round'. When Pierre beheld his neighbour next morning at dawn the first impression of him as something rotund was fully confirmed: Platon's whole figure—in a French military coat belted round the waist with rope, a soldier's cap and bast shoes—was round. His head was as round as a ball; his back, his chest, his shoulders, even his arms, which he always held as though he were about to embrace something, were round; his pleasant smile and his large gentle brown eyes were round, too.

Platon Karatayev must have been on the far side of fifty to judge by his stories of the campaigns he had taken part in as an old soldier. He himself had no idea, and could never have determined with any accuracy, how old he was. But his shining white, strong teeth, which showed in two unbroken semicircles whenever he laughed —which was often—were all sound and good; there was not a grey hair in his beard or on his head, and his whole physique gave an impression of suppleness and of unusual hardiness and endurance.

His face, in spite of a multitude of curving wrinkles, held an expression of innocence and youth; his voice had an agreeable sing-song note. But the chief peculiarity of his speech was its spontaneity and shrewdness. It was evident that he never considered what he had said or was going to say, and this lent an especial and irresistible persuasiveness to the quick, true modulations of his voice.

His physical strength and agility during the first period of his imprisonment were such that he seemed not to know what fatigue or sickness meant. Every night before going to bed he repeated: 'O Lord, lay me down like a stone and raise me up like new bread;' and when he got up in the morning he would give his shoulders a certain shake and say: 'Lie down and curl up, get up and shake up.' And indeed he had only to lie down to fall asleep like a stone, or give himself a shake and be ready without a second's delay for any sort of work, just as children are ready for their toys directly they open their eyes. He knew how to do everything, not particularly well but not badly either. He could bake, cook, sew, carpenter and cobble boots. He was always busy, and only at night allowed himself to indulge in conversation, which he loved, and singing. He sang not as a trained singer does who knows he is being listened to, but like the birds, obviously because he was as much obliged to give vent to those sounds as one sometimes is to stretch oneself or move about; and his singing was always light, sweet, plaintive, almost feminine, and his face the while was very serious.

Being in prison, and having let his beard grow, he had apparently cast off everything alien and military that had been forced upon him, and unconsciously relapsed into his old peasant habits.

'A soldier away from the army is the shirt worn outside the breeches again,' he would say.

He did not like talking about his soldiering days, though he had no complaints to make and was proud of repeating that he had never once been flogged in all his years of service. When he had stories to tell they were generally of some old and evidently precious memory of the time when he lived the life of a *Kristianin*—a Christian—as he called it, instead of *krestianin*.[1] The proverbs of which he made so much use were not the mainly coarse and indecent expressions common among soldiers but the popular saws which taken without a context seem to have so little meaning, but which suddenly acquire a profoundly wise significance when applied appropriately.

He would often say the exact opposite of what he had said on a previous occasion, yet both would be right. He liked to talk and he talked well, adorning his speech with terms of endearment and proverbial sayings, which Pierre fancied he often invented himself; but the great charm of his stories lay in the fact that he clothed the simplest incidents—incidents which Pierre might easily have witnessed without taking any particular notice—in a grave seemliness to befit their nature. He liked listening to the folktales which one of the soldiers used to tell of an evening (they were always the same ones), but most of all he liked

[1] The Russian word for *peasant*—[Tr.]

to hear stories of real life. He would listen with a happy smile, now and then putting in a word or asking a question for the purpose of elucidating for himself the moral excellence of what was related to him. Karatayev had no attachments, friendships or loves, as Pierre understood them; but he felt affection for and lived on sympathetic terms with every creature with whom life brought him in contact, and especially with man—not any particular man but those with whom he happened to be. He loved his dog, loved his comrades and the French, loved Pierre who was his neighbour; but Pierre felt that for all Karatayev's warm-heartedness towards him (thus involuntarily paying tribute to Pierre's spiritual life) he would not suffer a pang if they were parted. And Pierre began to feel the same way about Karatayev.

In the eyes of the other prisoners Platon Karatayev was just an ordinary soldier like the rest of his kind. They called him 'Little falcon' or 'Platosha', chaffed him good-naturedly and sent him on errands. But to Pierre he always remained what he had seemed that first night—an unfathomable, rounded-off, eternal personification of the spirit of simplicity and truth.

Platon Karatayev knew nothing by rote except his prayers. When he opened his mouth to speak he appeared to have no idea how, having once begun, he would finish up.

Sometimes Pierre, struck by the force of his remarks, would ask him to repeat them, but Platon could never recall what he had said a moment before, just as he could never tell Pierre the words of his favourite song. *Mother, little birch-tree* and *my heart is sick* came in but they made no coherent sense. He did not understand and could not grasp the meaning of words apart from their context. Every utterance and action of his was the manifestation of a force uncomprehended by him, which was his life. But his life, as he looked at it, held no meaning as a separate entity. It had meaning only as part of a whole of which he was at all times conscious. His words and actions flowed from him as smoothly, as inevitably and spontaneously as fragrance exhales from a flower. He could

20

not understand the value or significance of any word or deed taken separately.

War and Peace, Book IV, Part 1, ch. xiii.

This is not Pierre's first impression of him. He first saw Karatayev in the shed on the previous evening when he was merely described as a little man with a soft, respectful voice. Pierre accepted a baked potato from him with some salt taken out of a rag and he was so hungry that it tasted better than any food he had ever eaten. But he was too tired to take much notice of the man who gave it to him.

The emphasis on roundness in the second paragraph is such that it becomes almost symbolical. Everything about Karatayev is rotund, ample, and the mention of unbroken semi-circles and curving wrinkles in the third paragraph adds unobtrusively to this impression of roundness while the stress on the teeth helps to emphasise the fact that he smiles a lot.

The significance of the character for Pierre creeps in under cover of this overwhelming physical impression. He is an embodiment of naturalness. His life, his mind, his reactions have all the simplicity in them that Pierre finds enviable and inimitable. But there is nothing idealistic about Tolstoy's presentation of the peasant. He is no reincarnation of Rousseau's noble savage. His imperfections are realistically highlighted. He does nothing particularly well but he has a self-sufficiency which Pierre lacks, and needs. His wisdom, such as it is, is the wisdom of folk sayings and it is only in this particular ambience that Pierre would find himself quite so attracted to it. Imprisonment in these conditions brings out the lowest common multiple in humanity. Conditioned, even to the extent that he has been, by life in high society, Pierre finds himself ignorant of the best way to eat a baked potato in his hands, but he could not whole-heartedly wish to resemble Karatayev more, even though he now feels in many ways his inferior.

Above all it is Karatayev's spontaneity which Pierre admires. Each moment, each experience is separate from every other moment or experience and each reaction is fresh and free. He can even contradict himself with impunity; he is right each time. Emotionally he has no ties, which allows him to enjoy each moment of comradeship without feeling any regrets at parting. To a man plagued by ambivalence and conflicting loyalties as Pierre is, the attraction of Karatayev is easily understandable. Tolstoy portrays him through Pierre's eyes and his importance is that of a kind of anti-self. He is everything that Pierre is not, and the experience of knowing him and liking him has its effect on Pierre.

In a sense, Karatayev represents a stage through which Pierre passes quite late in his spiritual odyssey. In the same sense, Princess Lisa, Andrei's wife, represents a stage in Andrei's development which he is already moving away from when we first meet him. Here is Tolstoy's first description of her:

3

The young Princess Bolkonsky had brought some work in a gold-embroidered velvet bag. Her bewitching little upper lip, shaded with the faintest trace of down, was rather short and showed her teeth prettily, and was prettier still when she occasionally drew it down to meet the lower lip. As is always the case with a very charming woman, this little imperfection—the shortness of the upper lip and her half-open mouth—seemed to be a special form of beauty peculiarly her own. Everyone enjoyed seeing this lovely young creature so full of life and gaiety soon to become a mother and bearing her burden so lightly. Old men and dull and dispirited young men felt as though they had caught some of her vitality after being in her company and talking to her for a little while. Whoever spoke to her and saw the bright little smile accompanying every word and the constant gleam of her white teeth was sure to go away thinking that he had been unusually amiable that day. And it happened the same with everyone.

Swaying slightly, the little princess tripped round the table, her work-bags on her arm, and gaily arranging the folds of her gown seated herself on a sofa near the silver samovar, as if all that she was doing was a *partie de plaisir* for herself and everyone around her.

'I have brought my work,' she said in French, opening her reticule and addressing the company generally. 'Mind you don't let me down, Annette,' she turned to her hostess. 'You wrote that it was to be an informal little evening, so you see what I have got on.'

And she spread out her arms to display her elegant grey dress trimmed with lace and girdled with a wide ribbon just below the bosom.

'*Soyez tranquille, Lise,* you will always be prettier than anyone else,' replied Anna Pavlovna.

'You know,' Lisa went on in French and in the same tone of voice, addressing a general, 'my husband is deserting me. He is going to get himself killed. Tell me what this nasty war is about,' she said, this time to Prince Vasili, and without waiting for an answer she turned to speak to his daughter, the beautiful Hélène.

'What an adorable creature the little princess is!' whispered Prince Vasili to Anna Pavlovna.

War and Peace, Book I, Part 1, ch. xii.

The writing makes no attempt to describe everything about the princess. It is an impressionistic picture : a few quick, broad, accurate strokes, concentrating on just one

23

or two features to produce the general effect that such a girl would produce on a roomful of people. We start from a fact—that she has brought some work to do in Anna Pavlovna's drawing room—proceed to a brief but strikingly vivid description and then we start seeing her through other people's reactions to her, so that in fact we are simultaneously seeing them, her and the effect that she has on them. That they have no apparent effect on her helps to make the point that she is wholly absorbed with the effect she is having on them.

Her bright, small-scale charm is evoked by her first line of dialogue and the hint is planted that in the most amiable way she is showing off under the guise of self-deprecation. Her mindlessness is established by the superficial question about 'this nasty war'—and by the way she does not wait for an answer. Tolstoy's irony is unobtrusive. He seems only to be stating what happened.

In the subsequent appearances of 'the little princess' references to her short upper lip keep recurring like *leitmotivs* in a Wagner opera. In the stoutness of pregnancy, 'her eyes and the short downy lip and its smile were curled up just as gaily and sweetly'. When Andrei returns from the war to find her dying in childbirth:

4

Strands of her black hair curled about her hot perspiring cheeks; her rosy delightful little mouth with its downy lip was open and she was smiling joyfully.

And when he goes into the room just over a page later to find her dead

despite the fixed eyes and the pallor of her cheeks there was the same expression as before on the charming child-like face with its upper lip shaded with fine dark hair.

24

Years later we hear that her son

grew up, changed, grew rosy, grew a crop of curly dark
hair, and without knowing, smiling and gay, raised the
upper lip of his well-shaped mouth just like the little dead
princess.

The plain Princess Maria is Andrei's sister:

5

The little princess got up from the arm-chair, rang for the
maid, and hastily and merrily began to think out what
her sister-in-law should wear and to put her ideas into
effect. Princess Maria's self-respect was wounded by the
fact that the arrival of a suitor could perturb her, and it
was still more mortifying that both her friends took her
agitation as a matter of course. To tell them that she felt
ashamed for herself and for them would be to betray her
agitation, while to decline to dress up as they suggested
would prolong their banter and insistence. She flushed,
her lovely eyes lost their brilliance, red blotches appeared
on her face, which took on the unbeautiful victimized
expression it so often wore, as she surrendered herself to
Mademoiselle Bourienne and Lisa. Both women laboured
with *perfect sincerity* to make her look pretty. She was
so homely that it could never have entered the head of
either of them to think of her as a rival. Consequently it
was with perfect sincerity, in the naïve, unhesitating con-
viction women have that dress can make a face pretty,
that they set to work to attire her.

'No, really, *ma bonne amie*, that dress is not becoming,'
said Lisa, looking sideways at Princess Maria from a distance. 'Tell her to bring out your maroon velvet. Yes,
really! Why, you know, this may be the turning-point of
your life. That one's too light, it doesn't suit you. No, it's
all wrong!'

It was not the dress that was wrong, but the face and
whole figure of the Princess Maria, but neither Mademoiselle Bourienne nor the little princess realized this:

they still fancied that if they put a blue ribbon in her hair and combed it up high, and arranged the blue sash lower on the maroon velvet, and so on all would be well. They forgot that the frightened face and the figure could not be altered, and therefore, however much they might vary the setting and adornment, the face itself would remain pitiful and plain. After two or three changes to which Princess Maria submitted meekly, when her hair had been arranged on the top of her head (a style which quite altered and spoilt her looks) and she had put on the maroon velvet with the blue sash, the little princess walked round her twice, with her small hand smoothing out a fold here and pulling down the sash there, and then gazed at her with head first on one side and then on the other.

'No, it won't do,' she said decidedly, clasping her hands. 'No, Marie, this dress really does not suit you at all. I like you better in your little grey everyday frock. Please, for my sake. Katya,' she said to the maid, 'bring the princess her grey dress, and you'll see, Mademoiselle Bourienne, how I'll arrange it,' she added, smiling in anticipation of artistic enjoyment.

But when Katya brought the required garment Princess Maria still sat motionless before the glass looking at her face, and in the mirror she saw that there were tears in her eyes and her mouth was quivering and she was on the point of breaking into sobs.

'Come, *chère princesse*,' said Mademoiselle Bourienne, 'just one more little effort.'

The little princess, taking the dress from the maid, went up to Princess Maria.

'Now, we'll try something simple and nice,' she said.

The three voices—hers, Mademoiselle Bourienne's and Katya's, who was laughing at something—blended into a sort of gay twitter like the chirping of birds.

'No, leave me alone,' said Princess Maria.

And there was such seriousness and such suffering in her tone that the twitter of the birds was silenced at once. They looked at the great beautiful eyes, full of tears and brooding, turned on them imploringly, and realized that it would be useless and even cruel to insist.

26

'At least alter your coiffure,' said the little princess. 'Didn't I tell you,' she added reproachfully to Mademoiselle Bourienne, 'Marie has one of those faces which that style never suits. Never. Do please rearrange it.'

'Leave me alone, leave me alone. I don't care in the least,' answered a voice scarcely able to keep back the tears.

Mademoiselle Bourienne and the little princess were obliged to acknowledge to themselves that Princess Maria in this guise looked very plain, far more so than usual, but it was too late. She was staring at them with an expression they both knew, thoughtful and sad. It did not frighten them (Princess Maria never inspired fear in anyone). But they knew that when this expression appeared on her face she became mute and inflexible.

'You will alter it, won't you?' said Lisa, and when Princess Maria made no answer Lisa went out of the room.

Princess Maria was left alone. She did not comply with Lisa's request, and not only did not rearrange her hair but did not even look at herself in the glass. Letting her arms drop helplessly, she sat with downcast eyes and day-dreamed. She imagined a husband, a man, a strong, commanding and mysteriously attractive being, suddenly carrying her off into a totally different happy world that was his. She pictured a child, *her own*—like the baby she had seen the day before in the arms of her old nurse's daughter—at her breast, with her husband standing by and gazing fondly at her and the child. 'But no, it can never be, I am too ugly,' she thought.

War and Peace, Book I, Part 3, ch. iii.

This time the main focus is on the plainness of a plain woman at the moment when she is about to meet a prospective husband and it therefore seems particularly important that she should look her best. The two women who are trying 'with *perfect sincerity*' to help her are

27

both pretty and the self-regarding complacency in their actions and remarks heightens the pathos. Tolstoy sympathises with Maria's patience and hopelessness. Again without a detailed description, we get a clear impression of what she looks like, particularly when red blotches appear on her face and when her mouth quivers. And we see how the dressing-up, which could be so intensely enjoyable for a girl who is even moderately good-looking, is a torture for her. Maria is characterised partly through the contrast with the two other women and it is appropriate that after seeing her through their eyes we penetrate into her day-dream about the husband and child.

Finally, here is our first encounter with Anna Karenina:

6

Vronsky followed the guard to the carriage, and at the door of the compartment had to stop and make way for a lady who was getting out. His experience as a man of the world told him at a glance that she belonged to the best society. He begged her pardon and was about to enter the carriage but felt he must have another look at her—not because of her beauty, not on account of the elegance and unassuming grace of her whole figure, but because of something tender and caressing in her lovely face as she passed him. As he looked round, she too turned her head. Her brilliant grey eyes, shadowed by thick lashes, gave him a friendly, attentive look, as though she were recognizing him, and then turned to the approaching crowd as if in search of someone. In that brief glance Vronsky had time to notice the suppressed animation which played over her face and flitted between her sparkling eyes and the slight smile curving her red lips. It was as though her nature was so brimming over with something that against her will it expressed itself now in a radiant look, now in a smile. She deliberately shrouded the light in her eyes but in spite of herself it gleamed in the faintly perceptible smile.

Vronsky stepped into the carriage. His mother, a wizened old lady with black eyes and ringlets, screwed up her eyes to scan her son and her thin lips smiled slightly. Getting up from her seat and passing her bag to her maid, she extended her little wrinkled hand to her son to kiss; then, lifting his head from her hand, she kissed him on the cheek.

'You got my telegram? You are quite well? That's a mercy.'

'Did you have a good journey?' asked her son, sitting down beside her and involuntarily listening to a woman's voice outside the door. He knew it was the voice of the lady he had met as he entered the coach.

'All the same I do not agree with you,' said the lady's voice.

'That's the Petersburg way of looking at it, madame.'

'Not at all, simply a woman's way,' she replied.

'Well, well, allow me to kiss your hand.'

'Good-bye, Ivan Petrovich. And would you see if my brother is here and send him to me,' said the lady right at the door now and coming back into the compartment again.

'Well, have you found your brother?' asked Vronsky's mother, addressing the lady.

Vronsky realized now that this was Madame Karenin.

'Your brother is here,' he said, rising. 'Excuse me, I did not recognize you. Our acquaintance was so short,' he said with a bow, 'that I am sure you do not remember me.'

'Oh yes,' she replied, 'I should have known you—your mother and I seem to have talked of nothing but you the whole journey,' she said, at last allowing the animation which she had been trying to suppress reveal itself in a smile. 'But still no sign of my brother.'

'Do go and call him, Aliosha,' said the old countess.

Vronsky stepped out on to the platform and shouted: 'Oblonsky! Here!'

But Madame Karenin did not wait: as soon as she

caught sight of her brother she jumped down from the
carriage with a light, sure step. Directly her brother
reached her, she flung her left arm round his neck with
a gesture that struck Vronsky by its decision and grace,
and drawing him quickly to her, kissed him warmly.
Vronsky did not take his eyes off her and, without knowing why, smiled. But recollecting that his mother was
waiting for him, he went back into the carriage.

'She is very charming, isn't she?' said the countess of
Madame Karenin. 'Her husband put her in with me and
I was delighted to have her. We talked the whole way.
So you, I hear . . . *vous filez le parfait amour. Tant
mieux, mon cher, tant mieux.*'[1]

'I do not know what you mean, *maman*,' replied her
son coldly. 'Well, shall we go?'

Madame Karenin entered the carriage again to say
good-bye to the countess.

'Well, Countess, you have met your son, and I my
brother,' she said gaily. 'And I had come to the end of all
my gossip and should have had nothing more to tell you.'

'Oh no,' said the countess, taking her hand. 'I could
travel round the world with you and never be dull. You
are one of those sweet women with whom it is nice to be
silent as well as to talk. Now please don't fret over your
son; you cannot expect never to be parted.'

Madame Karenin stood still, holding herself extremely
erect, her eyes smiling.

'Anna Arkadyevna has a little son of eight, I believe it
is,' explained the countess, 'and this is the first time they
have ever been parted, and she is fretting at having left
him behind.'

'Yes, we have been talking about our sons the whole
time, I of mine and the Countess of hers,' said Madame
Karenin, and again a smile illuminated her face, a caressing
smile intended for him.

'It must have been very boring for you,' he said,
promptly catching the ball of coquetry she had thrown

[1] . . . are living love's young dream. Good, my dear, I'm very
glad.

30

him. But apparently she did not care to pursue the conversation in that strain, and she turned to the old countess:

'Thank you so much. The time has passed so quickly. Good-bye, Countess.'

'Good-bye, my dear,' replied the countess. 'Let me have a kiss of your pretty little face. I can speak plainly at my age, so let me confess that I have lost my heart to you.'

Stereotyped as the expression was, Madame Karenin obviously took it seriously and was delighted. She blushed, bent down slightly, and put her cheek to the countess's lips. Then she drew herself up again and, with the same smile hovering between lips and eyes, gave her hand to Vronsky. He pressed the little hand offered to him, and the energetic grip with which she boldly and vigorously shook his filled him with joy, as if it were something special. She walked rapidly away, carrying her rather full figure with extraordinary lightness.

'Very charming,' said the old countess.

Her son thought so too. His eyes followed her till her graceful form was out of sight, and still the smile lingered on his face. Through the carriage window he saw her go up to her brother, put her arm in his, and start talking eagerly to him about something—something which obviously had no connexion with him, Vronsky, and he found that vexing.

'Well, and how are you, *maman*, quite well?' he asked a second time, turning to his mother.

Anna Karenina, Part 1, ch. xviii.

Although this is our first glimpse of Anna (after seventy-five pages of the novel) and although it seems at first to be Vronsky's first meeting with her, it turns out not to be, so that Tolstoy gets the advantages both of describing the impact she makes on Vronsky as if he were seeing her for the first time and of proceeding to carry them further forward into their relationship than they could possibly have gone (at this period, in this society) if they were total strangers.

Instead of describing her as he did Yeroshka, Tolstoy at first gives us nothing but Vronsky's fleeting impression of her face, and this impression is coloured as much by her animation as by her beauty. Already, in this first prophetic paragraph, there are indications that instinct and conscious intention are flowing in two contrary directions. The light in her eyes works against the willpower that tries to shroud it.

Vronsky is instantly so taken with her that he cannot help listening to her voice outside the carriage while he talks to his mother. It is only when Anna comes back inside that he realises who she is and she realises who he is, and now she no longer withholds the smile she had wanted to give him before. The characterisation of Anna continues in the description of her movements as she goes to greet her brother. We see these movements partly through the eyes of Vronsky who, momentarily forgetting his mother, finds himself smiling.

Anna comes back again to say goodbye to the old countess, who has obviously enjoyed her company, and in establishing the existence of Anna's young son, the countess's remark also carries an introductory hint of the closeness of the relationship between them. The phrases 'caressing smile'—it is typical of Tolstoy to define the quality of a smile—and 'ball of coquetry' indicate a tentative sexual attraction between Anna and Vronsky; it is a neat modulation to make the old lady profess that she has 'lost her heart' to the younger woman and ask for a kiss from that pretty little face. Anna blushes delightfully as she complies and the same smile stays on her face as she gives Vronsky her hand. The second reference to the lightness of her gait and the first to the fullness of her figure tell us what visual image stays with Vronsky as she moves away.

The whole episode is over in three pages but already the relationship between the two of them is under way: Tolstoy could not have laid a better foundation for what is to follow. Two pages later, when a railwayman gets killed under a train and Anna, trembling and hardly able to hold back her tears, says that it is a bad omen, we know that it is not only the accident which is ominous.

Group scenes

In these six extracts, the foreground has been shared
between at most three characters. In the next three
extracts, we have a wider field of vision and a bigger
group of protagonists.

7

Having ridden up to the highest point of our right flank,
Prince Bagration began to make the descent to the spot
where there was a continual racket of musketry and nothing could be seen for the smoke. The nearer they got to
the hollow the less they could see but the more they felt
the proximity of the actual battlefield. They began to
meet wounded men. One man with a bleeding head and
no cap was being dragged along by two soldiers who sup-
ported him under the arms. There was a rattle in his
throat and he vomited blood: the bullet must have hit
him in the mouth or throat. Another whom they met was
walking sturdily along by himself, without his musket,
groaning aloud and shaking his arm which had just been
injured, while the blood streamed down over his great-
coat as from a bottle. He looked more scared than hurt:
he had been wounded only a moment ago. Crossing a

road they descended a steep incline and saw a number of men lying on the ground; they also met a crowd of soldiers, some of whom were not wounded. The soldiers were climbing the hill, breathing heavily and, despite the general's presence, talking loudly and gesticulating. Farther forward in the smoke rows of grey cloaks were now visible, and an officer catching sight of Bagration rushed after the retreating throng of men shouting to them to come back. Bagration rode up to the ranks along which shots crackled out swiftly, now here, now there, drowning the sound of voices and the shouts of command. The whole atmosphere reeked with burnt explosives. The men's excited faces were black with powder. Some were using their ramrods, others putting powder on the touch-pans or taking charges from their pouches, while still others were firing, though what they were firing at could not be seen for the fog which there was no wind to carry away. Quite often there was a pleasant buzz and whistle. 'What is going on here?' wondered Prince Andrei, riding up to the crowd of soldiers. 'It can't be the line, for they are all crowded together. It can't be a charge because they are not moving. It cannot be a square for they are not drawn up for that.'

The commander of the regiment, a rather thin, frail-looking old man with an amiable smile and eyelids that drooped more than half-way over his old eyes, giving him a mild expression, rode up to Bagration and welcomed him as a host welcomes an honoured guest. He explained to Prince Bagration that his regiment had had to face a cavalry attack of the French, that though the attack had been repulsed he had lost more than half his men. The colonel said that the attack had been repulsed, supposing this to be the proper military term for what had happened; though in point of fact he did not know himself what had taken place during that half-hour to the forces entrusted to his command, and was unable to say with certainty whether the attack had been thrown back or whether his regiment had been worsted. All he knew was that at the beginning of the engagement balls and shells began flying all about his regiment and hitting his

35

men, then someone had shouted 'Cavalry!' and our side had started to fire. And they were still firing, not now at the cavalry which had disappeared, but at the French infantry who had shown themselves in the hollow and were shooting at our men. Prince Bagration inclined his head, to signify that this was all he could wish and just what he had forseen. Turning to his adjutant he ordered him to bring down the two battalions of the 6th Chasseurs whom they had just passed. Prince Andrei was struck at that instant by the change that had come over Bagration's face, which now wore the concentrated, happy look of determination of a man taking a final run before plunging into the water on a hot day. The dull lethargic expression was gone, together with the affectation of profound thought: the round, steady, hawk's eyes looked before him eagerly and somewhat disdainfully, apparently not resting anywhere although his movements were as slow and deliberate as before.

The regimental commander turned to Prince Bagration urging him to go back as it was too dangerous where they were. 'Please, your Excellency, for God's sake!' he kept repeating, glancing for support to the officer of the suite, who looked away from him. 'There, you see!' and he drew attention to the bullets perpetually buzzing, singing, and whistling around them. He spoke in a tone of entreating and protest such as a joiner might use to a gentleman picking up an axe: 'We're used to it, sir, but you'd blister your fine hands.' He spoke as if those bullets could not kill him, and his half-closed eyes lent still more persuasiveness to his words. The staff-officer joined his entreaties to those of the colonel but Prince Bagration made no reply and merely gave an order to cease firing and re-form, so as to give room for the two battalions approaching to join them. While he was speaking a breeze sprang up and like an invisible hand drew the curtain of smoke hiding the hollow from right to left, and the hill opposite with the French moving about on it opened out before them. All eyes instinctively fastened on this French column advancing against them and winding down over the rough ground. Already the soldiers' shaggy caps could be seen; already the officers could be distinguished from the men, and the standard flapping in folds against the staff.

'They march well,' remarked someone in Bagration's suite.

The head of the column had already descended into the hollow. The clash then would take place on this side of the dip. . . .

The remains of our regiment which had already been in action hastily re-formed and moved to the right; from behind it, dispersing the laggards, came the two battalions of the 6th Chasseurs in fine order. They had not yet reached Bagration but the heavy measured tread could be heard of a whole body of men marching in step.

War and Peace, Book I, Part 2, ch. xviii.

Just before this passage Prince Andrei has been listening to the conferences between the general, Prince Bagration, and the commanding officers serving under him, and it has become apparent that Bagration is not really in control of what is going on. Instead of giving clear orders, he just lets things happen, afterwards trying to make it look as though they happened in accordance with his plans. His only real contribution is as a paternal influence which calms the men who have lost their nerve and encourages the more spirited to act courageously.

In the portrait of chaos contained in this excerpt, Tolstoy narrates first from Bagration's viewpoint, then from Andrei's, then from Bagration's again. We ride over the battlefield with him, hearing the noises and seeing what can be seen through the smoke. In the description of the wounded men, the narrative picks on individual details of sight, sound and smell which contribute effectively to the general picture.

It is a desire to impress Bagration that makes the officer

37

try to rally his retreating men. Andrei, as a spectator, cannot see any pattern or purpose in the chaos that surrounds him. Even the men who are firing or using their ramrods do not seem to know the object of what they are doing. The colonel who makes his report to Bagration does not know whether his men have repulsed the enemy or been worsted by them, and Bagration's reaction is equally meaningless.

The fog-like smoke and the whistling bullets add to the impression of highly dangerous confusion and when the breeze disperses the smoke, the French column is seen to be advancing menacingly. The shaggy caps and the heavy sound of marching steps are the only physical details we get but they are enough to give point and immediacy.

8

There was a sudden stir: a whisper ran through the assembly, which pressed forward and then back, separating into two rows down the middle of which walked the Emperor to the strains of the orchestra which struck up at once. Behind him came his host and hostess. He entered rapidly, bowing to right and left as if anxious to get through the first formalities as quickly as possible. The band played the polonaise in vogue at the moment on account of the words that had been set to it, beginning: 'Alexander, Elisaveta, our hearts ye ravish quite . . .' The Emperor passed on into the drawing-room; the crowd surged to the doors; several persons dashed backwards and forwards, their faces transformed. The wave receded from the doors of the drawing-room, where the Emperor appeared engaged in conversation with his hostess. A young man, looking distraught, bore down on the ladies, begging them to move away. Several ladies, with faces betraying complete disregard of all the rules of decorum,
38

squeezed forward to the detriment of their toilettes. The men began to select partners and take their places for the polonaise.

Space was cleared, and the Emperor, smiling, came out of the drawing-room leading his hostess by the hand but not keeping time to the music. The host followed with Maria Antonovna Naryshkin; and after them ambassadors, ministers and various generals, whom Madame Peronsky diligently named. More than half the ladies had partners and were taking up or preparing to take up their positions for the polonaise. Natasha felt that she would be left with her mother and Sonya among the minority who lined the walls, not having been invited to dance. She stood with her slender arms hanging by her sides; her scarcely defined bosom rising and falling regularly, and with bated breath and glittering, frightened eyes gazed straight before her, evidently equally prepared for the height of joy or the depths of misery. She was not interested in the Emperor or any of the great personages whom Madame Peronsky was pointing out—she had but one thought: 'Can it be that no one will come up to me, that I shall not be among the first to dance? It is possible that not one of all these men will notice me? They don't even seem to see me, or if they do they look as if they were saying, "No, she's not the one I'm after, it's no use looking at her!" No, it cannot be,' she thought. 'They must know how I am longing to dance, and how splendidly I dance, and how much they would enjoy dancing with me.'

War and Peace, Book II, Part 3, ch. xvi.

The occasion is in great contrast to that of the previous excerpt but the narrative method is similar: without stopping for a deliberate survey of the area of action, Tolstoy keeps it impressionistically alive in the background while he focuses on the movement in the fore-

39

ground. As the Emperor moves, we learn what is going on around him, but this time everything is seen from outside. The narrative does not adopt the viewpoint of any of the characters until it settles on Natasha, profiting from the contrast between the ceremony of imperial majesty and a young girl's nervousness that no one is going to ask her to dance. The transition to her and her preoccupations is accomplished very smoothly by picking on her as an exception to the dancers who are taking up their positions for the polonaise. (This is typical of Tolstoy's method of isolating his heroes from their social context—when we first meet Pierre at Anna Pavlovna's fashionable reception, it is his social blunders which make him stand out from the rest.) The physical details about Natasha—slender arms, scarely defined bosom, bated breath, glittering frightened eyes—make her more vivid than the Emperor and bring her decisively into the foreground.

Tolstoy uses a very different, more Dickensian technique in *Resurrection* when he describes the cell in the women's prison. First the room itself is briefly and directly pictured, then the grouping of the women in it and then the prisoners themselves. Unlike Dostoyevsky, Tolstoy had no first-hand experience of prison life and he does not aspire to a documentary approach. He paints the scene in human pigments—by characterising the prisoners.

9

Maslova's cell was a long room about twenty feet long and sixteen wide, with two windows, a big stove from which the plastering was peeling off, and some wooden bunks which occupied two-thirds of the floor space. In the middle of the room, opposite the door, hung a dark-

coloured icon with a wax taper and a dusty bunch of ever-
lasting flowers fastened to it. Behind the door, on the
dark, rotten floor to the left, stood a vile-smelling tub. The
roll had just been called and the women were shut in for
the night.

This cell was occupied by fifteen persons—twelve
women and three children.

It was still quite light and only two of the women were
lying on the bunks. One was an idiot who had been
imprisoned because she had no passport; she spent most
of the time sleeping, with a prison cloak drawn over her
head. The other, a consumptive, was serving a sentence
for theft; she was not asleep but lay with wide-open eyes,
the prison cloak folded under her head, doing her best to
keep from coughing as the phlegm rose in her throat and
choked her. The rest of the women, bareheaded and with
nothing on but coarse unbleached linen gowns, either sat
on the bunks and sewed, or stood idly by the window
gazing out into the yard at the passing convicts. Of the
three who were sewing, one was the same old woman,
Korablyova, who had seen Maslova off when she left the
cell that morning. She was a tall, powerful, austere-look-
ing woman with a flabby double chin, a hairy mole on
her cheek, and gray-brown hair braided into a small, tight
pigtail. She had been sentenced to penal servitude for killing her husband with an ax because she found him impor-
tuning her daughter. She was orderly of the cell and carried on a small trade in drink. She wore spectacles, and
in her large sinewy hand she held a needle the way
peasants do, grasping it with three fingers, the point aimed
at her breast. The woman who sat next to her, making
coarse linen bags, was a little creature with a pug nose,
sallow skin, and small black eyes, kind and talkative. She
had been employed as signal woman on the railway. One
day she was not at her post, no flag was shown, an accident occurred, and she was sentenced to three months'
imprisonment. The third woman who was sewing—her
companions called her Fenichka, but her name was really
Fedosya—was young and attractive. Her cheeks were
rosy and her eyes were blue. Her thick brown hair was

coiled in two plaits round her small head. She had attempted to poison her husband. It happened very soon after their marriage, when she was only sixteen. While she was on bail awaiting her trial, a reconciliation took place, and eight months afterwards, when the trial was about to begin, they were living together—as tender and devoted a couple as could be found. Her husband and his parents —his mother particularly, who had become very fond of the girl—moved heaven and earth to obtain her acquittal, but it was of no use. She was sentenced to hard labour in Siberia. This good-natured, cheerful girl, her face always wreathed in smiles, had her bunk next to Maslova, of whom she had grown so fond that she did everything she could to make her comfortable. Two other women sat on the bunks doing nothing. One seemed about forty years old, probably a handsome woman in her youth, but now very pale, worn, and emaciated. She was nursing a child. One day, in the village where she lived, a young recruit was seized—illegally conscripted, so the peasants thought —and when the villagers stopped the police officer and released their comrade, this woman—an aunt of the recruit—had been the first to catch hold of the bridle of the horse on which they were taking him away. The other woman, who seemed to have nothing to do, was a small, humpbacked, gray-haired, kindly old woman. She was pretending to catch a chubby four-year-old boy with closely clipped hair who was running to and fro, laughing happily. He had nothing on but a shirt, and every time he passed her he cried out, 'You didn't catch me that time!' This old woman and her son had been arrested on a charge of arson. She bore her imprisonment with the utmost patience, troubled only about her son who was in the same jail, and still more about her old husband; she was sure he was being devoured by vermin, since her daughter-in-law had gone away and there was no one to keep him clean.

Besides these seven women, there were four others who stood by one of the open windows, leaning on the grating and exchanging remarks with the passing convicts—the same gang that had encountered Maslova. One of these women, who was serving a sentence for theft, was a large, flabby, freckled creature with red hair and a double chin that hung over her unbuttoned neckband. She kept calling to the men in the yard, shouting out unseemly words in a loud, rough voice. Beside her stood an awkward, dark-skinned woman, no bigger than a child of ten, with a long body and short legs. Her face was covered with reddish blotches, her black eyes were set wide apart and, as she burst into shouts of laughter at what went on in the yard, her thick lips parted to reveal large white teeth. This prisoner, nicknamed 'Horoshavka'[1] for her love of finery, was to be tried for theft and arson. Behind them, dressed in a dirty gray linen gown, stood a thin, pregnant woman, looking very wretched; she had been arrested for concealing stolen goods. She stood there without speaking, but her smile showed that she was also enjoying the goings on in the yard. The fourth woman at the window was a peasant, short and stout, with prominent eyes and a kindly face, accused of selling spirits without a licence. She was the mother of the little boy who was playing with the old woman, and of a seven-year-old girl. As there was no one at home to take care of the children, she had been allowed to bring them with her. She stood near the window, knitting a stocking and glancing out from time to time; she frowned and closed her eyes, apparently in reproof of the unseemly talk. But her seven-year-old daughter, with loose flaxen hair, clothed only in a shirt, stood clutching the red-headed woman's gown with her thin little hand, and with wide-open eyes listened greedily to all the bad words, repeating them softly to herself as if she were learning them by heart. The twelfth prisoner was a sub-deacon's daughter, a tall and stately girl, who had drowned her baby in a well. Her loosely braided hair hung in disorder around her face; she wore a dirty gown and her feet were bare. She took no notice of anything that went on, but just paced up and down the room, her eyes fixed in a dull and glassy stare.

Resurrection, Book I, ch. xxx.

[1] Formed from a Russian word meaning 'to adorn oneself.'

This prepares the ground admirably for the fight between the red-haired woman and Korablyova, which comes only a few pages later.

10

'I'll tell you just what you've got to do, Katerina,' she began. 'In the first place you must write it down on paper that you're not satisfied with the sentence, and send that to the prosecutor.'

'What business have you got around here?' cried Korablyova, in an angry voice. 'You smell vodka, that's why you're so interested. We know what to do without your advice.'

'What's the matter with you? I'm not talking to you!'

'It's a drink you want, isn't it? That's why you're so nice all at once.'

'Well, give her some,' said Maslova, who was always giving things away.

'I'll give her something she won't like—'

'Let's see you do it,' began the red-haired one, advancing towards Korablyova. 'D'you think I'm afraid of you?'

'You prison scum!'

'And what are you?'

'You skinful of guts!'

'A skinful of guts, am I?—You murderess!' shouted the red-haired woman.

'Now, you just keep away from me,' said Korablyova, savagely.

But the red-haired woman was beyond warning; she pushed forward, and Korablyova hit her on her heavy breasts. It was as though the red-haired woman had been waiting for that signal. Out flew one hand and grabbed Korablyova by the hair, the other was aimed to strike her in the face. Korablyova warded off the blow while Maslova and Horoshavka tried to pull the red-haired woman away, but she had a firm hold of Korablyova's plait and would not let go. Only for an instant did she relax her grip, and then it was to twist the hair more tightly around her fist. Meanwhile, Korablyova, holding her head sideways, was battering the red-haired woman in the chest and trying to bite the hand tearing out her hair. All the other women crowded around the combatants, screaming and doing their best to separate them. Even the consumptive drew near and stood coughing as she watched the fight. The children huddled together, crying.

Presently, hearing the noise, the warden and the matron came in and separated them. Korablyova unbound her gray plaits and the loose hair that had been torn out fell to the floor. The red-haired woman tried to pull her ragged gown together. Both shouted loudly, complaining and trying to explain what had happened.

'It's vodka that's at the bottom of all this!' said the matron. 'Tomorrow I shall report you to the inspector. He'll attend to you. I can smell it! You'd better get rid of it if you know what's good for you. We've no time to listen to your stories now. Go to your bunks and keep quiet!'

But it was a long time before they could be reduced to silence. Across the room the women kept shouting at each other about how it had all begun and whose fault it was. At last the warder and the matron went away, and the women, calming down, began to get ready for bed. The old woman stood before the icon and said her prayers.

'Aah—you convicts!' came the hoarse voice of the red-haired woman from the other end of the room; she accompanied her words with extraordinary complicated swearing.

'You'd better look out for yourself, or you'll catch it again,' retorted Korablyova, with a train of similar abuse.

Then both relapsed into silence.

'If they hadn't interfered, I'd have scratched your old eyes out!' began the red-haired one again, and again Korablyova retorted in kind.

Then came a longer interval of silence, followed by fresh abuse. However, the intervals grew longer and longer, and finally all was quiet.

Most of the women were in bed; some were snoring; the

45

only ones still up were the old woman bowing before the icon (she always spent a long time over her prayers) and the subdeacon's daughter who, as soon as the warders had left, got up and began again to pace the room.

Maslova was not asleep. She was thinking to herself: 'Now I am really a convict,' for she had been called so twice: once by Bochkova and again by the red-haired woman. She could not get used to the idea.

Korablyova, who had been lying with her back towards her, now changed her position.

'I never dreamed I should come to this,' said Maslova, in a low voice. 'Other people do far worse things than I ever did, and they get away free while I have to suffer for a crime I never committed.'

'Don't be so downhearted, girl! Siberia isn't death—people manage to get on there. You'll survive it,' said Korablyova, trying to comfort her.

'I know I'll survive it. Still, it's hard. I didn't deserve this.'

'You can't go against the will of God,' said Korablyova, with a sigh. 'You can't go against Him!'

'I know that, aunty, but it's hard all the same.'

They were silent for a while.

'Here, listen to that wretch!' said Korablyova, calling Maslova's attention to a strange sound coming from the opposite end of the cell.

It was the suppressed sobbing of the red-haired woman. She was crying over the beating she had had and the vodka that she hadn't—vodka she wanted badly. And then she cried because her whole life had been one succession of abuse, jeers, insults, and blows. She tried to comfort herself by remembering her first sweetheart, a factory hand called Fedka Molodenkov, but when she thought of this, she also had to think how it ended. Molodenkov had rubbed vitriol on the most sensitive spot of her body when he was drunk, and had made a joke of it with his mates while she writhed in agony. She thought of this and was full of pity for herself. Thinking that no one could hear, she began to cry aloud, as children do, sniffling and swallowing her salt tears.

'You can't help feeling sorry for her,' said Maslova.
'No, of course you can't; but she's got to behave herself.'

Resurrection, Book I, ch. xxxii.

The effectiveness of this depends largely on the emotional switch to the weeping, which by making us identify more with the women, makes us more willing to believe in the violence which has just been described.

Inner and outer landscape

Tolstoy had a great talent for scenic description but very little interest in it. It is only in his early works that we find passages like this, from *Boyhood*:

II

The slanting rain driven by the violent wind pours down as from a bucket; the water streams down the back of Vassily's frieze coat into the muddy pools that have collected on the apron. The dust, which at first had been beaten into little pellets, was transformed into liquid mud which stuck to the wheels; the jolts became fewer and streams of turbid water flowed along the clayey ruts. The lightning grew paler and more diffuse and the rolling of the thunder sounded less awful when heard through the monotonous downpour.

But now the rain abates, the thunder-cloud begins to divide itself into fleecy cloudlets and grow lighter where the sun should be, and a patch of clear blue is visible through the light-grey edges of the cloud. A minute later a shy sunbeam glistens in the puddles along the road, on the long lines of rain now falling thin and straight as from a sieve, and on the shining newly-washed grass by the roadside. A great cloud still lours black and threatening as ever on the far horizon but I am not afraid of it now. I experience an inexpressible joyous feeling of optimism which rapidly replaces my oppressive sensation of dread. My soul smiles, like Nature refreshed and rejoicing. Vassily turns down the collar of his cloak, takes off his cap and shakes it. Volodya throws back the apron. I lean out of the chaise and eagerly drink in the fresh and fragrant air. The shining well-washed body of the carriage with its boxes and portmanteaux sways along in front of us; the horses' backs, the harness, the reins, the tyres on the wheels are all wet and glitter in the sun as if they had just been varnished. On one side of the road a vast field of winter grain, intersected here and there by shallow channels, its wet earth and vegetation shining bright, stretches away like a shadowy carpet to the very horizon; on the other side an aspen grove with an undergrowth of nut-bushes and wild cherry stands as if in an excess of happiness, without a rustle, while sparkling drops of rain slowly drip from its clean-washed branches on to last year's dry leaves. Crested skylarks circle all about us with glad songs and downward swooping. Small birds flutter and bustle in the dripping bushes, and from the heart of the wood the clear note of the cuckoo reaches our ears. So bewitching is the wonderful fragrance of the wood after that early spring storm—the fragrance of birch-trees, violets, rotting leaves, mushrooms and the wild cherry— that I cannot stay in the chaise. So I jump from the step and run towards the bushes, and though raindrops shower over me I break off wet branches of the flowering wild cherry, stroke my face with them and revel in their glorious scent.

Boyhood, ch. ii.

Later, he angles his narrative so strongly on the fore-ground that we only get such minimal and impressionistic glimpses of the background as we absolutely need. Whereas a novelist like Balzac delights in giving detailed graphic descriptions of the houses his characters live in, Tolstoy barely mentions the architecture or even the atmosphere of the big houses in which the main scenes of *War and Peace* and *Anna Karenina* are set.

But just as he aimed at describing a button left half undone in terms of a character's inner life, his chief interest in landscape is in its correlation with the inner landscape. A good example is in the scene in *Anna Karenina* where Levin, who has been working on the hay-harvest with his peasants, spends a night on top of a haystack trying to resolve his problems. He has been particularly impressed by the newly-married couple Vanka Parmenich and his wife and by the way they work together. He has also enjoyed the peasants' merrymaking but been unable to join in it.

12

The singing women were drawing nearer Levin and he felt as if a thunder-cloud of merriment were swooping down upon him. The clouds swooped down and enveloped him; and the haycock on which he was lying, the other haycocks, the carts, the whole meadow and the distant fields all seemed to advance and vibrate and throb to the rhythm of this madly-merry song with its shouting and whistling and clapping. Levin felt envious of this health and mirthfulness, and longed to take part in this expression of joy at being alive. But he could do nothing except lie and look on and listen. When the peasants and their song had disappeared out of sight and hearing, a weary feeling of despondency at his own isolation, his physical inactivity, his alienation from this world, came over him.

Some of the very peasants who had most disputed with him over the hay—whom he had been hard on or who had tried to cheat him—those very peasants had nodded happily to him, evidently not feeling and unable to feel any rancour against him, any regret, any recollection even of having intended to cheat him. All that had been swallowed up in the day of cheerful common toil. God gave the day, God gave the strength for it. And the day and the strength were consecrated to labour, and that labour was its own reward. For whom the labour? What would be its fruits? These were idle considerations beside the point.

Levin had often admired this life, had often envied the men who lived it; but to-day for the first time, especially under the influence of what he had seen of the relations between Vanka Parmenich and his young wife, the idea came into his mind that it was in his power to exchange the onerous, idle, artificial, and selfish existence he was leading for that busy, honourable, delightful life of common toil.

The old man who had been sitting beside him had gone home long ago; the peasants had all dispersed. Those who lived near had ridden home, while those from a distance had gathered into a group for supper and to spend the night in the meadow. Levin, unnoticed by them, still lay on the haycock, looking round, listening, and thinking. The peasants who had remained for the night in the meadow scarcely slept all the short summer night. At first Levin heard merry chatter and general laughter over supper, then singing again and more laughter. The whole long day of toil had left upon them no trace of anything but gaiety.

Before dawn all grew quiet. Only the sounds of night were heard—the incessant croaking of frogs in the marsh and the horses snorting in the mist rising over the meadow before the morning. Rousing himself, Levin got up from the haycock and, looking at the stars, he saw that the night was over.

'Well, then, what am I going to do? How am I to set about it?' he said to himself, trying to put into words all he had been thinking and feeling in that brief night. All the thoughts and feelings he had passed through fell into three separate trains of thought. The first was the renunciation of his old life, of his utterly useless education. The idea of this renunciation gave him satisfaction, and was easy and simple. Another series of thoughts and mental images related to the life he longed to live now. The simplicity, the integrity, the sanity of this life he felt clearly, and he was convinced he would find in it the content, the peace, and the dignity, of the lack of which he was so painfully conscious. But the third line of thought brought him to the question of how to effect this transition from the old life to the new. And here nothing was clear. 'Take a wife? Have work and the necessity to work? Leave Pokrovskoe? Buy land? Join a peasant community? Marry a peasant girl? How am I to set about it?' he asked himself again, and could find no answer. 'I haven't slept all night, though, and can't think it out now,' he said to himself. 'I'll work it out later. One thing is certain : this night has decided my fate. All my old dreams of family life were nonsense, not the real thing,' he told himself. 'It's all ever so much simpler and better . . .

'How beautiful!' he thought, looking up at some fleecy white clouds poised in the middle of the sky right above his head, like a strange mother-of-pearl shell. 'How lovely everything is in this lovely night! And when did that shell have time to form? I was looking at the sky a moment ago and only two white streaks were to be seen. Yes, and my views of life changed in the same imperceptible way!'

He left the meadow and walked along the highway towards the village. A slight breeze was blowing up and it became grey and overcast with the moment of gloom that usually precedes daybreak and final victory of light over darkness.

Shrinking from the cold, Levin walked fast, with his eyes fixed on the ground.

'What's that? Someone coming,' he thought, catching the jingle of bells, and lifting his head. Forty paces from him a four-in-hand with luggage on top was driving towards him along the grassy high-road on which he was walking. The wheelers pressed in towards the pole away from the ruts, but the skilful driver, seated on one side of the box, kept the pole over the ruts, so that the wheels ran on the smooth part of the road.

That was all Levin noticed, and without wondering who it could be he glanced absently at the coach.

An elderly woman was dozing in one corner, while at the window, evidently only just awake, sat a young girl holding the ribbons of her white nightcap in both hands. Serene and thoughtful, full of a subtle, complex inner life, remote from Levin, she was gazing beyond him at the glow of the sunrise.

At the very instant when this vision was vanishing, the candid eyes fell on him. She recognized him, and a look of wonder and delight lit up her face.

He could not be mistaken. There were no other eyes like those in the world. There was only one creature in the world that could concentrate for him all the light and meaning of life. It was she. It was Kitty. He realized she must be on her way to Yergushovo from the railway station. And everything that had been stirring Levin during that sleepless night, all the resolutions he had made, all vanished at once. He recalled with disgust his ideas of marrying a peasant girl. There alone, in the rapidly disappearing carriage that had crossed to the other side of the road, was the one possible solution to the riddle of his life, which had weighed so agonizingly upon him of late.

She did not look out again. The sound of the carriage springs could no longer be heard, the jingle of bells grew fainter. The barking of dogs told him the carriage had reached the village, and all that was left were the empty fields, the village in the distance, and he himself, solitary and apart from it all, making his lonely way along the deserted high-road.

He looked up at the sky, expecting to find there the cloud-shell he had delighted in and which had seemed to him the symbol of the ideas and feelings of that night. There was nothing in the sky in the least like a shell now. There, in the remote heights above, a mysterious change had been accomplished. No trace was to be seen of the shell; but spread half across the sky was a smooth tapestry of fleecy cloudlets, growing tinier and tinier. The sky had turned blue and clear; and met with the same tenderness but with the same remoteness his questioning gaze.

'No,' he said to himself, 'however good that simple life of toil may be, I cannot go back to it. I love *her*.'

Anna Karenina, Part 3, ch. xii.

One of the many things which is striking about this passage is the way Tolstoy uses the movements of the clouds and the ebb and return of daylight. Like images in a well organised poem, these visual effects become very much more than visual effects. They help to articulate the statement Tolstoy is making about what is going on inside Levin. The peasants' merrymaking helps to define Levin's feeling of alienation and he longs intensely to be able to feel a part of their world, just as Olenin longed to become part of the Cossack community. But just as he seems on the point of committing himself to a binding decision, he looks up at the cloud-patterns, which change and reform with such speed that they seem like a comment on the speed of the shifts in his own *weltanschauung*. Kitty passing in her carriage is almost like a sun piercing through the clouds and his resolutions vanish like clouds. Looking up to find the shell-like shape that gave him so much pleasure he sees that the sky has almost cleared. When he tells himself that he loves her, it is not for the first time but Tolstoy's use of the clouds tells us that this time Levin has committed himself.

Master and Man is a story in which the weather and the landscape—or snowscape—act not only like poetic images but also as a major protagonist. In this passage, the master, Vasili Andreevich has abandoned his servant in the snow and ridden off on the horse.

13

Meanwhile Vasili Andreevich, with his feet and the ends of the reins, urged the horse on in the direction in which for some reason he expected the forest and the forester's hut to be. The snow covered his eyes and the wind seemed intent on stopping him, but bending forward and constantly lapping his coat over and pushing it between himself and the cold harness pad which prevented him from sitting properly, he kept urging the horse on. Mukhorty ambled on obediently though with difficulty, in the direction in which he was driven.

Vasili Andreevich rode for about five minutes straight ahead, as he thought, seeing nothing but the horse's head and the white waste, and hearing only the whistle of the wind about the horse's ears and his coat collar.

Suddenly a dark patch showed up in front of him. His heart beat with joy, and he rode towards the object, already seeing in imagination the walls of village houses. But the dark patch was not stationary, it kept moving; and it was not a village but some tall stalks of wormwood sticking up through the snow on the boundary between two fields, and desperately tossing about under the pressure of the wind which beat it all to one side and whistled through it. The sight of that wormwood tormented by the pitiless wind made Vasili Andreevich shudder, he knew not why, and he hurriedly began urging the horse on, not noticing that when riding up to the wormwood he had quite changed his direction and was now heading the opposite way, though still imagining that he was riding towards where the hut should be. But the horse kept making towards the right, and Vasili Andreevich kept guiding it to the left.

Again something dark appeared in front of him. Again he rejoiced, convinced that now it was certainly a village. But once more it was the same boundary line overgrown with wormwood, once more the same wormwood desperately tossed by the wind and carrying unreasoning terror to his heart. But its being the same wormwood was not all, for beside it there was a horse's track partly snowed over. Vasili Andreevich stopped, stooped down and looked carefully. It was a horse-track only partially covered with snow, and could be none but his own horse's hoofprints. He had evidently gone round in a small circle. 'I shall perish like that!' he thought, and not to give way to his terror he urged on the horse still more, peering into the snowy darkness in which he saw only flitting and fitful points of light. Once he thought he heard the barking of dogs or the howling of wolves, but the sounds were so faint and indistinct that he did not know whether he heard them or merely imagined them, and he stopped and began to listen intently.

Suddenly some terrible, deafening cry resounded near his ears, and everything shivered and shook under him. He seized Mukhorty's neck, but that too was shaking all over and the terrible cry grew still more frightful. For some seconds Vasili Andreevich could not collect himself or understand what was happening. It was only that Mukhorty, whether to encourage himself or to call for help, had neighed loudly and resonantly. 'Ugh, you wretch! How you frightened me, damn you!' thought Vasili Andreevich. But even when he understood the cause of his terror he could not shake it off.

'I must calm myself and think things over,' he said to himself, but yet he could not stop, and continued to urge the horse on, without noticing that he was now going with the wind instead of against it. His body, especially between his legs where it touched the pad of the harness and was not covered by his overcoats, was getting painfully cold, especially when the horse walked slowly. His legs and arms trembled and his breathing came fast. He saw himself perishing amid this dreadful snowy waste, and could see no means of escape.

Suddenly the horse under him tumbled into something and, sinking into a snow-drift, began to plunge and fell on his side. Vasili Andreevich jumped off, and in so doing dragged to one side the breechband on which his foot was resting, and twisted round the pad to which he held as he dismounted. As soon as he had jumped off, the horse struggled to his feet, plunged forward, gave one leap and another, neighed again, and dragging the drugget and the breechband after him, disappeared, leaving Vasili Andreevich alone in the snow-drift.

Master and Man, ch. viii.

Even here, though the external world of wind and snow is described quite realistically, Tolstoy frames his story in such a way that it is not at all separate from the character's inner world. The weather and the wormwood are part of Vasili Andreevich's terror and the terrifying cry turns out to be nothing but the neighing of a horse. The narrative is solidly anchored on prosaic details like the drugget and the breechband, but they get nightmarishly swallowed up in the all-embracing snow which becomes identical with the all-embracing terror.

Inner monologue

In Tolstoy's fiction, the basic ontological questions are never far from the surface. What is life about? How should we live it? What is the purpose of our existence? This is why so many of the key moments come when characters arrive at what seems like a new understanding of the problems or a new answer. These moments of revelation can't be shared. Even if the subject of them is with other people at the time, the experience is essentially solitary. It therefore can't be rendered in dialogue, only in some form of monologue.

There is an early instance in *The Cossacks* when Olenin, tracking a stag, crawls into a thicket and stretches out in the actual spot where the animal has lain.

14

He examined the dark foliage around him, the marks of sweat, the dry dung, the imprint of the animal's knees, the lump of black earth it had kicked up, and his own footprints of the day before. He felt cool and comfortable. He was not thinking about anything in particular, or wishing for anything. Suddenly there came over him such a strange feeling of overwhelming happiness and universal love that he began to cross himself as he did when a child, and murmur words of gratitude. With extraordinary clearness he started thinking: 'Here am I, Dmitri Olenin, a being quite distinct from every other being, now lying all alone heaven knows where—where a stag lived, an old stag, a beautiful stag, who perhaps has never seen a man; in a place where no human being has ever been before, or thought these thoughts. Here I sit, with trees young and old around me, one of them festooned with wild vines; and pheasants soar in the air about me, chasing each other and perhaps scenting their dead brothers.' He picked up his pheasants, examined them and wiped the warm blood off his hand on to his coat. 'Maybe the jackals sniff the smell of blood, and retire with disappointed faces. Everywhere around me, flying in and out among the leaves, which must seem to them like vast islands, mosquitoes hang and buzz in the air: one, two, three, four, a hundred, a thousand, a million mosquitoes, all for some reason making their buzzing noise near me, and each one of them as distinct and separate a Dmitri Olenin as I am.' Then he imagined he knew what the gnats were thinking and buzzing about. 'Here, this way, lads! Here's something good to eat,' they hum as they settle down upon him. And it was clear to him that he was not a Russian nobleman at all, a member of Moscow society, friend and relation of this person and that, but simply another mosquito or pheasant or stag like the mosquitoes, pheasants and stags having their haunts in the woods around him. 'Just like them, just like old Yeroshka, I shall live my little life and then die. And as he quite truly said: Grass will grow over me, and that will be all.

'But even if the end is grass growing over me,' his thoughts ran on, 'still I must live, and be happy, because happiness is all I desire. It doesn't matter what I am—an animal like all the rest over which the grass will grow and that will be the end, or a particle of Divinity—I must still live in the best possible way. How, then, must I live so as to be happy, and have I not been happy hitherto?' And he began to review his past life, and to feel disgust at himself. He saw himself as terribly exacting and selfish, although in reality wanting for nothing. And while he looked at the green leaves with the light shining through them, at the sun coming low in the clear sky, happiness suffused him as before. 'What makes me so happy and what did I live for until now?' he asked himself. 'How exacting I have been for my own interests, how I worried and schemed, yet all I gained was shame and sorrow. And now I find I don't need anything to make me happy!' And suddenly it seemed as though a new world were revealed to him. 'Now I know what happiness is,' he said to himself. 'Happiness lies in living for other people. And that's evident. The desire for happiness is innate in every human being: therefore it must be intended. Attempts to satisfy it selfishly—by pursuing wealth, fame, material well-being or love—may come to nothing, for circumstances may deny them. It follows, then, that it is these pursuits *per se* that are wrong: not the craving for happiness. What then are the cravings that can always be satisfied, independently of external circumstances? What are they? Love for others, and self-sacrifice.' He was so pleased and excited at this discovery, which seemed to him a new truth, that he sprang to his feet and began impatiently thinking to whom he could sacrifice himself, whom he could do good to, and love, immediately. 'Since I need nothing for myself,' he kept thinking, 'why not devote my life to others?'

The Cossacks, ch. xx.

Prince Andrei's inner monologue on his death-bed seems, in part, to be a dialogue with Natasha but in fact she adds very little to what he says:

15

Prince Andrei not only knew he was going to die but felt
that he was dying, that he was already half dead. He felt
remote from everything earthly and was conscious of a
strange and joyous lightness in his being. Neither impatient nor anxious, he awaited what lay before him.
That sinister, eternal, unknown and distant something
which he had sensed throughout his life was now close
upon him and—as he knew by the strange lightness of
being that he experienced—almost comprehensible and
tangible. . . .

In the past he had dreaded the end. Twice he had experienced the frightful agony which is the fear of death,
of the end, but now that fear meant nothing to him.

The first time was when the shell was spinning like a
top before him, and he had looked at the stubble-field, at
the bushes, at the sky, and known that he was face to
face with death. When he had recovered consciousness
after his wound, and instantly, as though set free from
the cramping bondage of life, the flower of eternal un-
fettered love had opened out in his soul, he had had no
more fear and no more thought of death.

During the hours of solitude, suffering and half-delirium
that he spent after he was wounded, the more deeply he
penetrated this new principle of eternal love which had
been revealed to him, the more he unconsciously detached
himself from earthly life. To love everything and every-
body, always to sacrifice self for love, meant to love no
one in particular, meant not to live this mundane life.
And the more imbued he became with this principle of
love, the more he let go of life and the more completely
he annihilated that fearful barrier which—in the absence
of such love—stands between life and death. Whenever,
during that first period, he remembered that he had to
die, he said to himself: 'Well, what of it? So much the
better!'

But after the night at Mytishchy when, half delirious,
he had seen her for whom he longed appear before him,

61

and pressing her hand to his lips had wept soft, happy tears, love for one particular woman had stolen unobserved into his heart and bound him again to life. And glad and agitating thoughts began to occupy his mind. Recalling the moment at the ambulance-station when he had seen Kuragin, he could not now regain the feeling he had then. He was tormented by the question: 'Is he alive?' And he dared not inquire.

His illness pursued its normal physical course, but what Natasha referred to when she said 'This suddenly happened' had occurred two days before Princess Maria's arrival. It was the last spiritual struggle between life and death, in which death gained the victory. It was the unexpected realization that life, in the shape of his love for Natasha, was still precious to him, and a last, though ultimately vanquished, onslaught of terror before the unknown.

It happened in the evening. As usual after dinner he was slightly feverish, and his thoughts were preternaturally clear. Sonya was sitting at the table. He fell into a doze. Suddenly he was conscious of a glow of happiness.

'Ah, she has come!' he thought.

And so it was: in Sonya's place sat Natasha who had just crept noiselessly in.

Ever since she had begun looking after him he had always had this instinctive awareness of her presence. She was sitting in a low chair placed sideways so as to screen the light of the candle from him, and was knitting a stocking. (She had learned to knit after Prince Andrei had casually remarked that no one made such a good sick-nurse as an old nanny who knitted stockings, and that there was something soothing about knitting.) The needles clicked in her swiftly moving fingers, and then he could see quite clearly the pensive profile of her bent head. She shifted a little, and the ball of wool rolled from her lap. She started, glanced round at him, and shading the candle with her hand stooped carefully with a supple, precise movement, picked up the ball and sat back as before.

He watched her without stirring and saw that she

62

wanted to draw a deep breath after picking up the wool, but refrained from doing so and breathed cautiously.

At the Troitsa monastery they had spoken of the past, and he had told her that if he lived he would always thank God for his wound, which had brought them together again; but since then they had never mentioned the future.

'Could it be, or could it not?' he was wondering now as he looked at her and listened to the light click of the steel needles. 'Can fate have brought us together so strangely only for me to die? . . . Can the truth of life have been revealed to me only to give my whole life the lie? I love her more than anything in the world! But what am I to do if I love her?' he said to himself, and he involuntarily groaned, from a habit he had fallen into in the course of his sufferings.

Hearing the sound, Natasha laid down her stocking, leaned nearer to him and suddenly, noticing his shining eyes, went up to him with a light step and bent over him.

'You are not asleep?'

'No, I have been looking at you a long time. I felt you come in. No one else gives me that sweet sense of tranquillity . . . that radiance. I could weep for joy.'

Natasha moved closer to him. Her face shone blissful with happiness.

'Natasha, I love you too much. More than anything in the world.'

'And I?' She turned away for a second. 'But why too much?' she asked.

'Why too much? . . . Well, what do you think, what do you feel in your heart—in your heart of hearts: am I going to live? What do you think about it?'

'I am sure of it, sure of it!' Natasha almost shouted, seizing both his hands in hers with a passionate gesture.

He was silent awhile.

'How good that would be!'—and taking her hand he kissed it.

Natasha felt happy and deeply stirred; but at once

63

remembered that this would not do and that he must be kept quiet.

'But you have not slept,' she said, subduing her joy. 'Try and sleep . . . please!'

He pressed her hand and let it go, and she moved back to the candle and sat down again in the same position as before. Twice she glanced round at him and met his shining eyes fixed on her. She set herself a stint on the stocking and resolved not to look round till she had finished it.

He did, in fact, soon shut his eyes and fall asleep. He did not sleep long, and woke with a start and in a cold perspiration.

As he fell asleep he was still thinking of the subject which now occupied his mind all the time—of life and death. And of death more than life. He felt nearer to death.

'Love? What is love?' he mused.

'Love hinders death. Love is life. Anything at all that I understand, I understand only because I love. Everything is—everything exists—only because I love. All is bound up in love alone. Love is God, and to die means that I, a tiny particle of love, shall return to the universal and eternal source.' These thoughts seemed comforting to him. But they were only thoughts. There was something lacking in them, they were confused and too one-sidedly personal, too intellectual. And he was a prey to the same restlessness and uncertainty. He fell asleep.

He dreamed that he was lying in the room in which he actually was lying, but that he had not been wounded and was quite well. Many various people, indifferent, insignificant people, appear before him. He is talking to them, arguing about some trifle. They are preparing to set off somewhere. Prince Andrei dimly realizes that all this is trivial and that he has other far more serious matters to attend to, but still he continues to speak, surprising them by empty witticisms. Gradually, imperceptibly, all these persons begin to disappear, to be replaced by a single question, that of the closed door. He gets up and goes towards the door in order to shoot the bolt and lock it. Everything depends on whether he can lock it quickly

64

enough. He starts, tries to hurry but his legs refuse to move and he knows he will not be in time to lock the door, yet he still frenziedly strains every effort to get there. Agonizing fear seizes him. And this fear is the fear of death: *It* stands behind the door. But while he is helplessly and clumsily stumbling towards the door that dreadful something is already pushing against it on the other side and forcing its way in. Something not human—death —is breaking in through the door and he must hold the door to. He grapples with the door, straining every ounce of his strength—to lock it is no longer possible—but his efforts are feeble and awkward, and the door, under the pressure of that awful thing, opens and shuts again.

Once more *It* pushes on the door from without. His last superhuman struggles are vain and both leaves of the door are noiselessly opened. *It* comes in, and it is *death*. And Prince Andrei died.

But at the very instant when in his dream he died Prince Andrei remembered that he was asleep, and at the very instant when he died he exerted himself and was awake.

'Yes, that was death. I died—and woke up. Yes, death is an awakening!' His soul was suddenly flooded with light, and the veil which till then had concealed the unknown was lifted from his spiritual vision. He felt as if powers hitherto confined within him had been set free, and was aware of that strange lightness of being which had not left him since.

War and Peace, Book IV, Part 1, ch. xvi.

In *The Death of Ivan Ilyich*, the monologue becomes more like a dialogue, but this time both voices are inside the old man's head:

16

He wept at his own helplessness, at his terrible loneliness, at the cruelty of man, the cruelty of God, at the absence of God.

'Why hast Thou done this? Why hast Thou brought me to this? Why, why dost Thou torture me so dreadfully?'

He did not expect any answer, and yet wept because there was no answer and could be none. The pain flared up more acutely again but he did not stir and did not call. He said to himself: 'Go on, smite me? But why? What have I done to Thee? What is it for?'

Then he was still and not only ceased weeping but even held his breath and became all attention: he listened, as it were, not to an audible voice but to the voice of his soul, to the tide of his thoughts that rose up within him.

'What is it you want?' was the first clear conception capable of expression in words that he heard. 'What is it you want? What is it you want?' he repeated to himself.

'What do I want? Not to suffer. To live,' he answered.

And again he listened with such concentrated attention that even his pain did not distract him.

'To live. Live how?' asked his inner voice.

'Why, to live as I used to—well and pleasantly.'

'As you used to live—well and pleasantly?' queried the voice. And he began going over in his imagination the best moments of his pleasant life. But oddly enough none of those best moments of his pleasant life now seemed at all what they had seemed at the time—none of them except his earliest memories of childhood. There, in childhood, there had been something really pleasant with which it would be possible to live if it could return. But the person who had experienced that happiness was no more: it was like a memory of someone else.

As soon as the period began which had produced the present Ivan Ilyich everything that had seemed a joy at the time now dwindled away before his eyes and was transformed into something trivial and often disgusting.

And the farther he departed from childhood and the nearer he came to the present, the more worthless and doubtful were the joys. This began from the time he was a law student. There was still something then that had been genuinely good—gaiety, friendship, hopes. But in the upper classes these good moments were already becoming rarer. Later on, during the first years of his official career, when he was in the service of the Governor, there were again some good moments: they were the memories of love for a woman. Afterwards it all became mixed up, and less and less of it was good. And the farther he went the less good he found.

His marriage . . . as gratuitous as the disenchantment that followed, and his wife's bad breath, and the sensuality, the hypocrisy! And that deadly official life and the preoccupation with money, a year of it, two years, ten, twenty, and always the same thing. And the longer it lasted the more deadly it became. 'As though I had been going steadily downhill while I imagined I was climbing up. And that is really how it was. In public opinion I was going up, and all the time my life was sliding away from under my feet . . . And now it's all done and I must die.

'But what is it all about? Why is it like this? It can't be —it can't be that life is so senseless and loathsome. And if it really has been so loathsome and senseless, why must I die and die in agony? There is something wrong!

'Maybe I did not live as I should,' the thought suddenly occurred to him. 'But how could that be, when I have always done my duty,' he answered himself, and immediately dismissed from his mind this, the sole solution of all the enigma of life and death, as something quite impossible.

The Death of Ivan Ilyich, ch. ix.

The revelation he achieves at the moment of dying is, as before, about altruism. But he's incapable of arriving at it until he has rejected his life as he has actually lived it.

17

Then he felt that someone was kissing his hand. He opened his eyes and looked at his son. He felt sorry for him. His wife came up to him. He looked at her. She was gazing at him with open mouth, the tears wet on her nose and cheeks, and an expression of despair on her face. He felt sorry for her.

'Yes, I am a misery to them,' he thought. 'They are sorry but it will be better for them when I die.' He wanted to say this but had not strength to speak. 'Besides, why speak, I must act,' he thought. With a look he indicated his son to his wife and said:

'Take him away . . . sorry for him . . . sorry for you too . . .' He tried to add 'Forgive me' but said 'Forego' and, too weak to correct himself, waved his hand, knowing that whoever was concerned would understand.

And all at once it became clear to him that what had been oppressing him and would not go away was suddenly dropping away on one side, on two sides, on ten sides, on all sides. He felt full of pity for them, he must do something to make it less painful for them: release them and release himself from this suffering. 'How right and how simple,' he thought. 'And the pain?' he asked himself. 'What has become of it? Where are you, pain?'

He began to watch for it.

'Yes, here it is. Well, what of it? Let the pain be.

'And death? Where is it?'

He searched for his former habitual fear of death and did not find it. 'Where is it? What death?' There was no fear because there was no death either.

In place of death there was light.

'So that's what it is!' he suddenly exclaimed aloud. 'What joy!'

The Death of Ivan Ilyich, ch. xii.

Dialogue

Tolstoy seldom uses dialogue without dovetailing commentary into it and insights into what at least one of the characters is thinking. If the passage of dialogue is at all extended, it is rarely balanced equally between the characters. One is nearly always more in the limelight than the others.

One of the few exceptions is this confrontation between Andrei and Pierre in *War and Peace*, which illuminates both men equally. They have just come back from a soirée.

18

Pierre, arriving first, went straight to Prince Andrei's study like one thoroughly at home, and at once, from habit, stretched himself out on a sofa, took from the shelf the first book that came to hand (it was Caesar's *Commentaries*) and leaning on his elbow began reading it in the middle.

'What have you done to Mademoiselle Scherer? She will be quite ill now,' said Prince Andrei, as he came into the study rubbing his small white hands together.

Pierre rolled his whole person over so that the sofa creaked, lifted his eager face to Prince Andrei, smiled and waved his hand.

'That *abbé* was very interesting, only he has got hold of the wrong end of the stick. To my thinking, permanent peace is possible but—I don't know how to put it . . . Not by means of a political balance of power.'

Prince Andrei was obviously not interested in such abstract conversation.

'My dear fellow, one can't everywhere and at all times say all one thinks. Come, tell me, have you made up your mind at last? Is it to be the cavalry or the diplomatic service?' he asked after a momentary silence.

Pierre sat up on the sofa with his legs crossed under him.

'Can you imagine it, I still don't know! Neither prospect smiles on me.'

'But you must decide on something. Your father's expecting it.'

At the age of ten Pierre had been sent abroad with an *abbé* as tutor, and had remained away till he was twenty. On his return to Moscow, his father had dismissed the *abbé* and said to the young man, 'Now you go to Petersburg, look round and make your choice. I agree to anything. Here is a letter to Prince Vasili, and here is money. Write and tell me all about everything, and I will help you in every way.' Pierre had already been three months trying to choose a career and had come to no decision. It was in regard to this choice of a career that Prince Andrei spoke to him now. Pierre rubbed his forehead.

'But he must be a freemason,' said he, meaning the *abbé* he had met at the party.

'That is all nonsense.' Prince Andrei pulled him up again. 'We'd better talk business. Have you been to the Horse Guards?'

'No, not yet, but here is an idea that occurred to me which I wanted to tell you. This war now is against Napoleon. If it were a war for freedom, I could have understood it, and I should have been the first to join the
70

army; but to help England and Austria against the greatest man in the world—that is not right. . . .'

Prince Andrei merely shrugged his shoulders at Pierre's childish talk. He assumed the air of one who really finds it impossible to reply to such nonsense; but it would in fact have been difficult to answer this naïve querying in any other way than Prince Andrei did answer it.

'If everyone would only fight for his own convictions, there would be no wars,' he said.

'And a very good thing that would be,' said Pierre.

Prince Andrei laughed.

'Very likely it would be a good thing, but it will never happen.'

'Well, what are *you* going to the war for?' asked Pierre.

'What for? I don't know. Because I have to. Besides, I am going . . .' He stopped. 'I am going because the life I lead here—is not to my taste!'

> *War and Peace*, Book I, Part I, ch. v.

The flashback to Pierre's past is integrated effortlessly into the conversation and Tolstoy's commentary helps to adumbrate the differences in outlook between the two young men, but the main points are made dramatically by the dialogue itself.

One example of a much less reciprocal conversation comes later on in the very funny scene when Prince Vasili, who has been trying unsuccessfully to bring Pierre to the point of proposing to his highly nubile daughter Hélène, solves the problem by behaving just as if he had proposed.

19

Prince Vasili frowned, twisting his mouth to one side, and

his cheeks began to twitch with the disagreeable, brutal expression characteristic of him. He shook himself, got up, threw back his head and with resolute steps walked past the ladies into the little drawing-room. Swiftly and with an assumption of delight he went up to Pierre. His face was so extraordinarily solemn that Pierre rose in alarm.

'Thank God!' said Prince Vasili. 'My wife has told me!' He put one arm round Pierre, the other round his daughter. 'My dear boy. . . . My little girl. . . . I am very, very pleased.' His voice trembled. 'I loved your father . . . and she will make you a good wife. . . . God bless you both!'

He embraced his daughter, then Pierre again, and kissed him with his malodorous mouth. Real tears moistened his cheeks.

'Princess, come here!' he called.

The princess came in, and she too wept. The elderly lady also put her handkerchief to her eye. Pierre was kissed, and several times he kissed the hand of the lovely Hélène. After a while they were left alone again.

'All this had to be and could not have been otherwise,' thought Pierre, 'so it's no use wondering whether it is a good thing or not. It is good at least in that it's definite and I am no longer tortured by doubts.' Pierre held his betrothed's hand in silence, watching her beautiful bosom as it rose and fell.

'Hélène!' he said aloud, and stopped.

'Something special is said on these occasions,' he thought, but could not for the life of him remember what it was. He glanced into her face. She bent forward closer to him. Her face flushed rosy-red.

'Oh, take off those . . . those . . .' she said, pointing to his spectacles.

Pierre took them off, and his eyes, besides the strange look people's eyes have when they remove their spectacles, held a look of dismay and inquiry. He was about to bend over her hand and kiss it, but with a quick, rough movement of her head she intercepted his lips and pressed them with her own. Pierre was struck by the transformed, unpleasantly distorted expression of her face.

'Now it's too late, it's all over; and besides I love her,' thought Pierre.

'*Je vous aime!*' he said, remembering what had to be said on these occasions; but the words sounded so thin that he felt ashamed for himself.

Six weeks later he was married and settled in the enormous newly-decorated Petersburg mansion of the Counts Bezuhov, the fortunate possessor, as people said, of a beautiful wife and millions of money.

War and Peace, Book I, Part 3, ch. ii.

In this whole passage, Pierre speaks four words. The initiative is first with the old prince and then with Hélène, but, as so often in Tolstoy, what a character thinks during a conversation can be more important than what he says. Pierre's thoughts are written out in dialogue form and, passive though he is in this scene, he is also unmistakably the chief protagonist. He is slow and confused but his freewill does operate and his decision is to accept the situation. The three blundering words he speaks in French confirm both the confusion and the decision.

It is interesting to compare this scene with Levin's proposal to Kitty in *Anna Karenina*, which, despite all its differences, is similar in coming very close to avoiding conversation. When the Prince, Kitty's father, leaves her alone with Levin, they talk, but only about the conversation they have just been listening to at the dinner table. Tolstoy's use of indirect speech to report this conversation emphasises the point that they are neither of them very interested in what they are saying—until their conversation comes to bear more closely on their own situation. At first Kitty very nearly walks out on Levin, and in his anxiety to stop her, he starts almost childishly improvising a game with the initial letters of words, half hoping

she will not understand what he is spelling out, half
scared that she will.

20

Scherbatsky left them, and Kitty, going up to a card-table,
sat down and, taking a piece of chalk, began drawing
diverging circles on the new green cloth.

They resumed the conversation started at dinner—the
emancipation and occupations of women. Levin agreed
with Dolly that a girl who did not marry could always
find some feminine occupation in the family. He sup-
ported this view by saying that no family can get along
without women to help them, that every family, poor
or rich, had to have nurses, either paid or belonging to the
family.

'No,' said Kitty, blushing, but looking at him all the
more boldly with her truthful eyes, 'a girl may be so
placed that it is humiliating for her to live in the family,
while she herself . . .'

He understood her allusion.

'Oh yes,' he said. 'Yes, yes, yes—you're right; you're
right!'

And he saw all that Pestsov had been driving at at
dinner about the freedom of women, simply because he
got a glimpse of the terror in Kitty's heart of the humiliation of remaining an old maid; and, loving her, he felt
that terror and humiliation, and at once gave up his contention.

A silence followed. She continued scribbling on the
table with the chalk. Her eyes shone with a soft light.
Surrendering to her mood he felt a continually growing ten-
sion of happiness throughout his whole being.

'Oh, I've scribbled all over the table!' she exclaimed,
and, putting down the chalk, made a movement to get up.

'What! Shall I be left alone—without her?' he thought,
with terror, and took the piece of chalk. 'Don't go,' he
said, sitting down at the table. 'I've wanted to ask you a
74

question for a long time.' He looked straight into her caressing, though frightened eyes.

'What is it?'

'Here,' he said, and wrote down the initial letters, w, y, t, m, i, c, n, b—d, t, m, n, o, t? These letters stood for, 'When you told me it could not be—did that mean never, or then?' There seemed no likelihood that she would be able to decipher this complicated sequence; but he looked at her as though his life depended on her understanding the words.

She gazed up at him seriously, then leaned her puckered forehead on her hand and began to read. Once or twice she stole a look at him, as though asking, 'Is it what I think?'

'I know what it is,' she said, flushing a little.

'What is this word?' he asked, pointing to the n which stood for *never*.

'That means *never*,' she said, 'but it's not true!'

He quickly rubbed out what he had written, handed her the chalk, and stood up. She wrote: T, I, c, n, a, d.

Dolly felt consoled for the grief caused by her conversation with Karenin when she caught sight of the two together: Kitty, with the chalk in her hand, gazing up at Levin with a shy, happy smile, and his fine figure bending over the table, his radiant eyes directed now on the table, now on her. He was suddenly radiant: he had understood. The letters meant: 'Then I could not answer differently.'

He glanced at her questioningly, timidly.

'Only then?'

'Yes,' her smile answered.

'And n . . . —and now?' he asked.

'Well, read this. I'll tell you what I should like, what I should like so much!' She wrote the initial letters: i, y, c, f, a, f, w, h, meaning, 'If you could forget and forgive what happened.'

He seized the chalk, breaking it with his nervous, trembling fingers, and wrote the first letters of the following sentence: 'I have nothing to forget and forgive; I have never ceased to love you.'

She looked at him with a smile that did not waver.

'I understand,' she said in a whisper.

He sat down and wrote a long sentence. She understood it all and, without asking if she was right, took the chalk and at once wrote the answer.

For a long time he could not make out what it was, and kept looking up into her eyes. He was dazed with happiness. He could not fill in the words she meant at all; but in her lovely eyes, suffused with happiness, he saw all he needed to know. And he wrote down three letters. But before he had finished writing she read them over his arm, and herself finished and wrote the answer, 'Yes.'

'Playing secrétaire?' said the old prince, coming up to them. 'But we ought to be going if you want to be in time for the theatre.'

Anna Karenina, Part 4, ch. xiii.

They are both very shy people and even after several years of marriage, when they quarrel over Levin's visit to Anna Karenina (who at the beginning of the story had caused Vronsky to jilt Kitty) the conversational clash is never a very direct one:

21

'We talk about the peasants drinking, but I really don't know who drinks most—the common people or our own class. The peasants drink at holiday times but . . .'

But Kitty was not interested in a dissertation on the drinking habits of the peasants. She had noticed his blush and wanted to know the reason for it.

'Well, and where did you go after that?'

'Stiva absolutely begged me to go and see Anna Arkadyevna.'

Saying this, Levin blushed still more, and his doubts as

to whether he had done right in going to call on Anna were finally solved. He knew now that he ought not to have gone.

Kitty's eyes opened wide and flashed at the mention of Anna, but she made an effort to conceal her agitation.

'Oh!' was all she said; and Levin was taken in.

'I'm sure you won't be angry with me for going. Stiva implored me to, and Dolly wished it,' Levin went on.

'Oh no!' she said, but he saw in her eyes a constraint that boded him no good.

'She is very charming, and a nice woman—very, very much to be pitied,' he said, telling her about Anna and her occupations and the message she had sent.

'Yes, of course she is much to be pitied,' Kitty remarked when he had finished. 'Who were your letters from?'

He told her, and misled by her quiet manner went to undress.

Coming back, he found Kitty still sitting in the same arm-chair. When he went up to her, she looked at him and burst into sobs.

'What is it? What is the matter?' he asked, well aware what the matter was.

'You have fallen in love with that hateful woman! She has bewitched you! I saw it in your eyes. Yes, yes! What will be the end of it? You were drinking and drinking at the club, and gambling, and then you went . . . to her, of all people! No, we must go away . . . I shall go away to-morrow.'

It was long before Levin could pacify his wife. At last he succeeded in calming her only by acknowledging that the wine he had drunk, together with his sense of pity, had been too much for him and he had succumbed to Anna's artful spell; and by promising that in future he would avoid her. He was sincerest of all when he confessed that living for so long in Moscow with nothing to do but eat, drink, and gossip was beginning to demoralize him. They talked till three o'clock in the morning. Only by three o'clock were they sufficiently reconciled to be able to go to sleep.

Anna Karenina, Part 7, ch. xi.

In *Resurrection* it is equally striking how seldom Tolstoy uses scenes of direct confrontation between Nekhludov and Maslova. It is Nekhludov's realisation of his own guilt, not anything that she says to him about it, that activates him and basically there is very little that she wants to say to him at any point of their complex relationship. This is part of the main point—that they both have so much effect on each other and so little contact. As their final conversation shows, they have achieved a rapport which does not require them to talk or even to be together :

22

'Have you been told that a mitigation of your sentence has been granted?'

'Yes, the inspector told me.'

'So when the document arrives you will be able to settle where you like. We will think it over—'

She interrupted him hastily.

'There's nothing to think over. I shall follow Vladimir Vassilievich wherever he goes.'

In spite of her excitement she looked straight into Nekhludov's eyes and spoke quickly and distinctly, as though she had learned a lesson.

'I see,' said Nekhludov.

'Well, Dmitri Ivanovich, if he wants me to live with him—' she paused, abashed, and corrected herself, 'wants me to be with him, I must consider myself lucky. What else is there for me—?'

'One of two things,' thought Nekhludov. 'Either she loves Simonson and has never required the sacrifice which I imagined I was making, or she continues to love me even while she refuses me for my own sake, and is burning her bridges by uniting her lot with Simonson's.' He felt ashamed of himself and knew that he was blushing.

'Of course, if you love him,' he said.

'Does it matter whether I do or not? I am past that

sort of thing. And, besides, Vladimir Vassilievich is a different kind of man.'

'Yes, of course,' began Nekhludov, 'he is a splendid fellow, and I think—' She interrupted him again as though she feared that he might say too much, or that she would not have a chance to say everything.

'You must forgive me, Dmitri Ivanovich, if I am not doing what you wish,' she said, looking straight at him with her mysterious squinting eyes. 'But this is how it had to be. You have your own life to live.'

She was only saying what he himself had just been thinking, but now he felt ashamed of the thought and regretted all that he would lose when he lost her.

'I did not expect this,' he said.

'Why should you live here and suffer?' she said, and smiled. 'You have suffered enough already.'

'I have not suffered. I have been happy and I should like to go on serving you if I could.'

'We,' she said, looking up at Nekhludov, 'we need nothing. You have already done a great deal for me. If it hadn't been for you—' She was about to say something more, but her voice quivered.

'I am the last person you should thank,' said Nekhludov.

'What's the use of trying to weigh up what we owe one another? God will make up our accounts,' she said and her black eyes shone with the tears that rushed into them.

'What a good woman you are!' he said.

'I? A good woman!' She smiled pitifully through her tears.

The Englishman interrupted. 'Can we get on?' he said.

'Just a moment,' said Nekhludov, and asked Katusha about Kryltzov.

She pulled herself together sharply and quickly told him what she knew. Kryltzov's journey had weakened him considerably and he had been sent straight to hospital. Maria Pavlovna was very anxious about him and had asked to be allowed to stay at the prison as a hospital nurse, but permission had not been granted.

79

'Shall I go now?' she asked, realizing that the Englishman was getting impatient.

'I will not say good-bye. I shall see you again,' said
Nekhludov, holding out his hand.

'Forgive me,' she whispered. Their eyes met, and by
her peculiar squinting look, her pitiful smile, and the
tone of her voice when she said, not 'Good-bye' but 'Forgive me,' Nekhludov understood. His second supposition
as to the cause of her decision was the real one. She loved
him and realized only too well that union with her
would ruin him. By remaining with Simonson she was
releasing him, and while rejoicing that in this way she
was accomplishing her purpose, she was yet mourning
that she must part from him. She pressed his hand and,
quickly turning, went from the room.

Nekhludov was now ready to go, but glancing at the
Englishman he saw he was still busily writing in his note-
book. Not wishing to disturb him. Nekhludov sat down
on the wooden seat by the wall and a great weariness
suddenly came over him. It was not the weariness one
feels after a sleepless night of travel or excitement—he
was terribly tired of life. He leaned back, closed his eyes,
and at once fell into a deep slumber.

'Would you also like to see the prisoners' cells?'

It was the inspector's voice. Nekhludov awoke suddenly, very surprised to find himself in the prison.

Resurrection, Book III, ch. xxv.

Satire and irony

Tolstoy's satire is chiefly directed against high society and there is very little of it in the early stories about family life. In *The Cossacks* he was enlarging his range by writing about a whole society instead of a small group of individuals, but it was such a primitive, unaffected society that no satirical deflation was called for.

His power of irony, however, can be seen growing in his early work and it grows directly out of his accurate observation of the co-presence of opposites. The more sharply the opposites are telescoped together, the more ironic the effect.

In *Childhood* the intention can barely be called ironical but there is a clear enjoyment of the discontinuity when the old nurse is made to switch from unbridled grief to careful store-keeping. She is speaking to Nikolai about his dead mother.

23

'Yes, my dear, she is here now looking at us and perhaps hearing what we are saying,' concluded Natalya Savishna.

And lowering her head she fell silent. Wanting a handkerchief to dry the falling tears, she got up, looked fixedly at me and in a voice trembling with emotion said:

'The Lord has brought me many degrees nearer to Him through this. What is there left for me here? Whom have I to live for? Who have I to love?'

'Don't you love us then?' I said reproachfully and hardly restraining my tears.

'The good God knows I love you, my duckies, but I never did and never can love anyone as I loved her.'

She could say no more but turned her head away and sobbed aloud. I no longer thought of sleep and we sat silently opposite one another and wept.

Foka came into the room. Seeing us like that and probably not wishing to disturb us, he stopped short at the door, looking at us timidly and not saying anything.

'What is it you want, Foka?' asked Natalya Savishna, wiping away her tears.

'A pound and a half of raisins, four pounds of sugar and three pounds of rice for the Kutya, please.'

'Here you are,' said Natalya Savishna, hurriedly taking a pinch of snuff and trotting briskly to the provision chest. The last traces of the grief aroused by our conversation vanished when she set about her duties, which she looked upon as of prime importance.

'Why four pounds?' she grumbled, getting out the sugar and weighing it on the balance. 'Three and a half will do,' and she took a few lumps from the scales.

Childhood, ch. xxviii.

The whole narrative of *War and Peace* is pervaded by a more conscious and complex irony. It is at work in many of the passages I have already quoted, such as the description of the little princess at Anna Pavlovna's party, the account of how she and Mademoiselle Bourienne help Princess Maria to dress and the battle scene in which the officer puts on a show of rallying his retreating men in order to impress Bagration and Bagration himself puts on a show of being more in control of events than he is. Tolstoy had a shrewd eye for the contradictions that were camouflaged by surface behaviour and the more he observed them, the riper his power of irony grew.

Some of the best examples of it are to be found in *Anna Karenina* where irony and satire often operate together.

24

Oblonsky never chose his tendencies and opinions any more than he chose the style of his hat or frock-coat. He always wore those which happened to be in fashion. Moving in a certain circle where a desire for some form of mental activity was part of maturity, he was obliged to hold views in the same way as he was obliged to wear a hat. If he had a reason for preferring Liberalism to the Conservatism of many in his set, it was not that he considered the liberal outlook more rational but because it corresponded better with his mode of life. The Liberal Party maintained that everything in Russia was bad; and in truth Oblonsky had many debts and decidedly too little money. The Liberal Party said that marriage was an obsolete institution which ought to be reformed; and indeed family life gave Oblonsky very little pleasure, forcing him to tell lies and dissemble, which was quite contrary to his nature. The Liberal Party said, or rather assumed, that religion was only a curb on the illiterate; and indeed Oblonsky could not stand through even the shortest church service without aching feet, or understand the point of all that dreadful, high-flown talk about the other world, when life in this world was really very pleasant. And then it sometimes amused Oblonsky, who liked a joke, to shock a conventional person with the suggestion that if one is going to pride oneself on one's birth, why stop short at Rurik and repudiate one's earliest ancestors

—the apes? Thus Liberalism had become a habit with Oblonsky and he enjoyed his newspaper, as he did his after-dinner cigar, for the slight haze it produced in his brain.

Anna Karenina, Part I, ch. iii.

Technically this is very adroit. The commentary and the implicit moral judgements are worked tightly into the factual description and though the satire is extremely damaging, it does nothing to disqualify Oblonsky from playing a primarily sympathetic role. He is stupid, shallow, confused and opportunistic but companionable, good-natured and good company.

There is irony of a different sort at work in the next passage where Anna, who is shortly to be unfaithful to Karenin, sympathises with Dolly over Oblonsky's infidelity.

25

'It is impossible to comfort me,' she said. 'Everything is finished now, after what has happened—it is all over!'

And directly she had said this, her face suddenly softened. Anna lifted Dolly's dry, thin hand, kissed it and said:

'But what is to be done, Dolly, what is to be done? What is the best thing to do in this dreadful situation? That is what we must consider.'

'Everything is at an end and there's nothing more to be said,' Dolly replied. 'And the worst of it is, you see, that I cannot cast him off: there are the children—I am tied. But I cannot live with him: it is torture for me to see him.'

'Dolly, my darling, he told me, but I want to hear it from you. Tell me all about it.'

84

Dolly looked at her inquiringly.

Unfeigned sympathy and love were written on Anna's face.

'If you like,' she said all at once. 'But I shall begin at the beginning. You know how I was married. With *maman's* upbringing, I was not merely innocent, I was stupid. I knew nothing. People say, I know, that husbands tell their wives about their past lives, but Stiva . . . Stepan Arkadyevich,' she corrected herself, 'told me nothing. You will hardly believe it, but until this happened I supposed I was the only woman he had ever loved. I lived thinking that for eight years. You see, it not only never entered my head to suspect him of being unfaithful to me—I believed such a thing to be impossible, and then . . . imagine what it was like with such ideas to find out all this horror, all this vileness. Try to understand. To be fully convinced of one's happiness, and suddenly . . .' continued Dolly, holding back her sobs, 'to find a letter . . . his letter to his mistress, my children's governess. No, it is too horrible!' She hurriedly drew out her handkerchief and hid her face in it. 'I can imagine being carried away by one's feelings,' she went on after a pause, 'but deliberately, slyly deceiving me . . . and with whom? . . . To go on being my husband together with her . . . that is horrible! You cannot understand . . .'

'Oh yes, I do understand! I do understand, Dolly dear, I do,' said Anna, pressing her hand.

'And do you imagine he realizes all the horror of my position?' continued Dolly. 'Not a bit! He is happy and contented.'

'Oh no!' Anna interrupted quickly. 'He's in a pitiful state, weighed down by remorse . . .'

'Is he capable of remorse?' broke in Dolly, scrutinizing her sister-in-law's face.

'Yes. I know him. I could not look at him without feeling sorry for him. We both know him. He's good-hearted, but he is proud, too, and now he feels so humiliated. What moved me most of all . . .' (and here Anna guessed what would touch Dolly most) 'he is tormented by two things: that he's ashamed for the children's sake

85

and that, loving you—yes, yes, loving you more than anything else in the world,' she went on hurriedly, to prevent Dolly from objecting, 'he has hurt and made you suffer. "No, no, she won't be able to forgive me," he keeps saying.'

Dolly gazed beyond her sister-in-law, listening thoughtfully.

'Yes,' she said, 'I realize that his position must be a terrible one—it is worse for the guilty than the innocent —if he knows he is the cause of all the misery. But how am I to forgive him, how can I be his wife again after her? For me to live with him now would be torture, just because I cherish my past love for him . . .'

And sobs cut short her words.

But as though by design, every time she was softened she began to speak again of what lacerated her.

Anna Karenina, Part i, ch. xix.

Tolstoy's mastery is such that, as in the description of the little princess, his irony can be at its deadliest when he seems merely to be giving an objective report of the facts.

He is at his most acid when he sums up the values of sympathetic but selfish men-of-the-world. Vronsky hardly emerges more favourably than Oblonsky:

26

Vronsky's life was particularly happy in that he had a code of principles, which defined with unfailing certitude what should and what should not be done. This code of principles covered only a very small circle of contingencies, but in return the principles were never obscure, and Vronsky, as he never went outside that circle, had

86

never had a moment's hesitation about doing what he ought to do. This code categorically ordained that gambling debts must be paid, the tailor need not be; that one must not lie to a man but might to a woman; that one must never cheat anyone but one may a husband; that one must never pardon an insult but may insult others oneself, and so on. These principles might be irrational and not good, but they were absolute and in complying with them Vronsky felt at ease and could hold his head high. Only quite lately, in regard to his relations with Anna, Vronsky had begun to feel that his code did not quite meet all circumstances and that the future presented doubts and difficulties for which he could find no guiding thread.

His present relations to Anna and to her husband were to his mind perfectly clear and simple. They were clearly and precisely defined in the code of principles which guided him.

She was an honourable woman who had bestowed her love upon him, and he loved her; therefore she was in his eyes a woman who had a right to the same, or even more respect than a lawful wife. He would have let his hand be cut off sooner than permit himself a word, a hint that might humiliate her, or fail to show her all the regard a woman could expect.

His attitude to society also was clear. Everyone might know or suspect it but no one must dare to speak of it. At the first hint he was ready to silence the speaker and make him respect the non-existent honour of the woman he loved.

Clearest of all was his attitude to her husband. From the moment that Anna gave Vronsky her love, he had considered his own right over her unassailable. Her husband was merely a superfluous person and a hindrance. No doubt he was in a pitiable position but how could that be helped? The only right a husband had was, weapon in hand, to demand satisfaction, and Vronsky had been prepared for that from the first moment.

But of late something new had arisen in his inner relations with Anna, which frightened Vronsky by their vagueness. Only the day before she had told him that she was with child. And he felt that this fact and what she expected of him called for something not fully defined in his code of principles. He had indeed been taken by surprise, and at the first moment when she told him of her condition his heart had prompted him to beg her to leave her husband. He had said so, but now, on reflection, he saw clearly that it would be better to manage without it; and yet while he told himself so, he was afraid that this might be wrong.

Anna Karenina, Part 3, ch. xx.

But he is most withering of all with religiose women:

27

The Countess Lydia had long given up being in love with her husband, but she had never ceased being in love with someone or other. She was in love with several people at once, both men and women; she had been in love with almost every person of note. She had lost her heart to each of the new princes and princesses who married into the Imperial family; she had been in love with a high dignitary of the Church, a vicar, and a parish priest; with a journalist, three slavophiles, with Komisarov, with a minister, a doctor, an English missionary, and Karenin. All these passions, ever waxing or waning, did not prevent her from keeping up the most extended and complicated relations with the Court and society. But from the day she took Karenin in his misfortune under her special protection, from the time when she began to busy herself in Karenin's household looking after his welfare, she had come to feel that all her other attachments were not the real thing, and that she was now genuinely in love, and with no one but Karenin. The feeling she now experienced for him seemed to her stronger than any she had ever had before. Analysing and comparing it with her previous loves, she saw clearly that she would never have been in love with Komisarov had he not saved the life of the Tsar, that she would never have been in love with Ristich-Kudzhitsky if there had been no Slavonic question; but that she loved Karenin for himself, for his lofty, uncomprehended soul, for the sweet—to her—high-pitched sound of his voice, for his drawling intonation, his weary eyes, his character, and his soft white hands with their swollen veins. She was not only overjoyed when they met, but she was always studying his face for signs of the impression she was making on him. She was anxious to please him, not merely by her conversation but by her whole person. For his sake she now lavished more pains on her dress than before. She caught herself day-dreaming as to what might have been, had she not been married and he been free. She blushed with excitement when he entered the room, she could not repress a smile of rapture when he happened to say something amiable to her.

Anna Karenina, Part 5, ch. xxiii.

Again satire and irony are both woven unobtrusively into the statement of the facts. The narrative strikes us as objective, quite without acrimony.

One of the signs of the inferiority of *Resurrection* to *War and Peace* and *Anna Karenina* is that in these two great novels, all strata of society and all characters, sympathetic and unsympathetic, seem to be sighted through the same ironically tinted lens, whereas in *Resurrection*, it is the rich and the powerful who are almost always the butts of satire, the poor and oppressed never. Not that all the convicts are sympathetic or all the officials unsympathetic, but in writing with such burning indignation about social injustice and in extending his range to give a more complete picture of non-aristocratic life than ever before, he found he had to wear bi-focal spectacles.

The satire against the aristocracy is harsher and cruder

than before. From what we see of Schoenbock, there is very little to choose between his moral fibre and Oblonsky's, but Tolstoy, like Nekhludov, gives him very short shrift.

28

He was hurrying along to overtake the carts when suddenly he heard a voice calling him. He stopped and saw, a few steps ahead of him, an officer with a pointed waxed mustache and smooth shining face, waving his hand from the smart droshky in which he sat, with a friendly smile revealing a row of remarkably white teeth.

'Nekhludov! Can it be you?'

At first Nekhludov felt delighted. 'Why—Schoenbock!' he exclaimed; but the next moment he knew that this was no occasion for delight. This was the same Schoenbock who had been to stay with his aunts. Nekhludov had not met him for some time. Rumours had reached him, however, that though heavily in debt he was still in his cavalry regiment and managed somehow to keep his place in the society of the wealthy. His gay, contented appearance seemed to corroborate this report.

'So glad I saw you! There isn't a soul in town,' he said, getting out of his droshky and straightening his shoulders. 'But you've grown old, my dear fellow! I only recognized you by your walk. Can't we dine together? Is there anywhere we can find a decent meal?'

'I am afraid I cannot spare the time,' said Nekhludov, trying to think of some way of escape that would not offend his former comrade. 'What are you doing here?' he asked.

'Business, my dear fellow, business; a matter of a trusteeship. I'm managing Samanov's affairs for him. Do you know him? He is tremendously rich, but his brain has gone soft. Imagine owning 130,000 acres!' he exclaimed with pride, as if he himself had made all that land. 'His affairs were in a very bad way. The entire estate was in the hands of the peasants. They cultivated the place and paid nothing in rent. They owed him eighty thousand rubles—just think of it!—but in one year I made a big change and increased the revenue by 70 per cent. What do you say to that?'

Nekhludov now remembered having heard that Schoenbock, who had spent all his own fortune, had through private influence been appointed trustee for the property of a rich old man who was squandering his estate. There could be no doubt that the trustee was getting on famously. 'How can I get away without offending him?' he kept wondering, as he looked at the plump face and pomaded moustache, and listened to the friendly chatter and bragging.

Resurrection, Book II, ch. x.

PART TWO

Subject matter

Subject matter

Tolstoy's range is enormous and already our extracts have taken us from the battlefield to the boudoir, from a women's prison to a ball with royalty present and through a rich variety of emotional relationships. As E. M. Forster suggested, one of Tolstoy's outstanding characteristics is the completeness of all his pictures—which makes it all the more difficult for any summary of them even to approximate to completeness. All I can hope to do in the remainder of this brief survey is to draw attention to a few contrasted areas of subject matter we have not already touched on.

Cossack women

In *The Cossacks* Tolstoy's subject is a relationship between an individual and a society. Olenin, the unsettled young nobleman, tries to root himself into a primitive community. As in the later novels, Tolstoy mixes fact and fiction, drawing on his memories of life in the Caucasus both in generalising about the Cossacks as a group and in individualising certain members of the group. There are passages of pure documentation, imparting information directly to the reader, and in the description of the Cossack women which follows the approach is sociological, almost anthropological.

29

The Cossack looks upon a woman as an instrument for his wellbeing. As long as she is single she is allowed to enjoy life but once married a wife must toil for her husband from her youth to the end of her days, and is expected to be as hardworking and submissive as an Oriental woman. In consequence the Cossack woman is powerfully developed both physically and morally, and though to all appearances in subjection possesses—as is usually the case in the East—incomparably greater influence and weight in family affairs than her Western sister. Their exclusion from public life and inurement to heavy manual labour give the women all the more authority and importance at home. The Cossack, who in the company of strangers considers it improper to speak affectionately or without reason to his wife, is very conscious of her superiority when they are alone. His house and all his property—in fact, the entire homestead—have been acquired and are kept together solely by her diligence and care. Though he is obstinately convinced that work is degrading to a Cossack, and is a proper occupation only for a Nogay labourer or a woman, he is vaguely aware of the fact that all he enjoys and calls his own is the result of that toil, and that although he considers both wife and mother his slaves, it lies in the power of the women to deprive him of all that makes life agreeable. Added to this, constant hard manual work and the responsibilities entrusted to them have endowed the Greben women with a peculiarly independent, masculine outlook and developed in them physical strength, common sense, resolution and stability of character to a remarkable degree. The women are in most cases stronger, more intelligent, more developed and handsomer than the men. The combination of the purest Circassian type of face with the broad and powerful build of the Northern woman makes the beauty of the Greben women particularly striking. Cossack women wear the Circassian dress: a Tartar smock, the *beshmet* and soft leather slippers; but they tie kerchiefs round their heads in the Russian fashion. Elegance, neatness and good taste in their dress and in the arrangement of their homes are a custom and a necessity with them. In their relations with men the women, and especially the unmarried girls, are completely free.

The Cossacks, ch. iv.

Polish soldiers showing their devotion to Napoleon

This passage occupies yet a different position in the no-man's-land between history and fiction. Most of the narrative is in the manner of reportage. Tolstoy writes nothing that an eye-witness could not have written about what happened. If the Colonel is described as being in dread of a refusal when he begs to be allowed to swim across the river, this is saying no more than anyone could have said who was watching the old man. Even at the end of the second paragraph, Tolstoy is hardly going further inside any character's thoughts than a casual observer could go but here, in this hint of what Napoleon is feeling, Tolstoyan irony comes into play.

30

The order was that they should look for a ford and cross the river. The colonel of the Polish Uhlans, a handsome old man, flushing and stammering in his excitement, asked the aide-de camp whether he might be permitted to swim the river with his men instead of seeking a ford. In obvious dread of a refusal, like a boy asking permission to get on a horse, he begged to be allowed to swim across

98

the river before the Emperor's eyes. The aide-de-camp replied that in all probability the Emperor would not be displeased at this excess of zeal.

No sooner had the aide-de-camp said this than the old whiskered officer, with beaming face and sparkling eyes, brandished his sabre in the air, shouted '*Vivat!*' and, calling on his men to follow him, spurred his horse and dashed down to the river. He gave a vicious thrust to his charger which had grown restive under him, and plunged into the water, heading for the deepest part where the current was swift. Hundreds of Uhlans galloped in after him. It was cold and forbidding in the middle in the rapid current. The Uhlans clung to one another as they fell from their horses. Some of the animals were drowned, some, too, of the men; the rest struggled to swim on and reach the opposite bank; and though there was a ford only about a quarter of a mile away they were proud to be swimming and drowning in the river under the eyes of the man who sat on the log and was not even looking at what they were doing. When the adjutant returned and, choosing an opportune moment, ventured to draw the Emperor's attention to the devotion of the Poles to his person, the little man in the grey overcoat got up and, having summoned Berthier, began pacing up and down the bank with him, giving him instructions and occasionally casting a glance of displeasure at the drowning Uhlans who distracted his thoughts.

War and Peace, Book III, Part 2, ch. i.

Historical theory

The Epilogue to *War and Peace* is divided into two parts. The first concludes the story; the second, if it were printed as a separate volume, would be classified by librarians as 'non-fiction'. It is a summary of Tolstoy's theory of history. After attempting in the main body of the novel to correct the generalisations of the historians by means of a complex of particularisations, he now attempts generalisations of his own.

31

What is the force that moves nations?

Biographical historians and historians of individual peoples understand this force as a power inherent in heroes and rulers. According to their chronicles events occur solely at the will of a Napoleon, an Alexander or in general the personages of whom they treat. The answers which historians of this *genre* return to the question of what force causes events to happen are satisfactory only so long as there is but one historian to each event. But as soon as historians of different nationalities and views begin describing one and the same event, the replies they give immediately lose all meaning, since this force is understood by them not only differently but often in absolutely opposite ways. One historian will maintain that a given event owed its origin to Napoleon's power; another that it was Alexander's power; while a third ascribes the event to the influence of some other person. Moreover, historians of this type contradict one another even in their interpretation of the force on which the authority of one and the same figure was based. Thiers, a Bonapartist, says that Napoleon's power was based on his virtue and his genius; Lanfrey, a Republican, declares that it rested on his rascality and skill in deceiving the people. So that the historians of this class, by mutually destroying one another's position, destroy the conception of the force which produces events, and furnish no reply to history's essential question.

Universal historians, who deal with all the nations, appear to recognize the erroneousness of the specialist historians' view of the force that produces events. They do not recognize it as a power pertaining to heroes and rulers but regard it as the resultant of a multiplicity of variously directed forces. In describing a war, or the subjugation of a people, the general historian looks for the cause of the event not in the power of any one individual but in the interaction of many persons connected with the event.

According to this view, the power of historical personages conceived as the product of several different forces can hardly, it would seem, be regarded as the force which in itself produces events. Yet general historians do almost invariably make use of the concept of power as a force which itself produces events and stands to events in the relation of cause to effect. We find them (the historians) saying at one minute that an historical personage is the product of his time and his power only the outcome of various forces; and at the next that his power is itself a force producing events. Gervinus, Schlosser and others, for instance, in one place argue that Napoleon was the product of the Revolution, of the ideas of 1789 and so forth, and in another plainly state that

the campaign of 1812 and other incidents not to their liking were simply the outcome of Napoleon's misdirected
will, and that the very ideas of 1789 were arrested in
their development by Napoleon's caprice. The ideas of
the Revolution and the general temper of the age produced Napoleon's power. But Napoleon's power stifled the
ideas of the Revolution and the general temper of the age.

War and Peace, Epilogue, Part 2, ch. ii.

Children

In *Childhood* Tolstoy drew directly on memories of his own childhood; in the episodes in *War and Peace* and *Anna Karenina* that involve children, he drew only indirectly. The scenes in *War and Peace* in which we see Natasha as a child contribute powerfully to the overall impression she is later to make on us as an adult: we forget neither the child she has been nor the extent to which she still is a child—the same child. Pierre is already an adult when we first meet him but Tolstoy makes us very aware that in part of his mind he has never grown up. We know him and like him better because of this.

But Tolstoy not only saw the child that survives in the adult. He also saw the adult in the child and in the scenes in *Anna Karenina* that involve Dolly's children or Anna's son Seriozha, he succeeds partly by identifying with the children's viewpoints exactly as if they were adults.

Dolly behaves in much the same way towards her children as she does towards everyone else. She is silly, impulsive, conventional, warm, anxious to do the right thing, uncertain what the right thing is. But highly critical of her though he is, Tolstoy is quite able to make her

CHILDREN

moving, especially when she is herself moved, as in this episode with her children.

32

On the way home the children were very quiet, feeling that something solemn had happened.

All went well at home, too; but at lunch Grisha began whistling and, what was worse, was disobedient to the English governess, and had to go without pudding. Dolly would not have let things go so far on such a day had she been present; but she was obliged to uphold the English governess, and confirmed her decision that Grisha should have no pudding. This rather spoiled the general happiness.

Grisha cried, declaring that Nikolinka had whistled, too, but they did not punish him, and that he was not crying about the pudding—he didn't mind that—but because it wasn't fair. This was too pathetic, and Dolly decided to speak to the governess and get her to forgive Grisha, and went to find her. But as she was passing the drawing-room she beheld a scene which filled her heart with such joy that tears came into her eyes and she pardoned the little delinquent herself.

The culprit was sitting in the corner by the window; beside him stood Tanya with a plate. On the plea of wanting to give her dolls some dinner, she had obtained the governess's permission to take her pudding to the nursery, and had brought it instead to her brother. Still weeping over the unfairness of his punishment, he was eating the pudding, and kept saying through his sobs, 'You have some too . . . let's eat it together . . . together.'

Tanya, affected at first by her pity for Grisha, and then by a sense of her own noble action, also had tears in her eyes; but she did not refuse, and ate her share.

When they caught sight of their mother, they were dismayed; but, looking into her face, they saw they were
104

not doing wrong, and with their mouths full, began to laugh and wipe their smiling lips with their hands, smearing their beaming faces all over with tears and jam.

Anna Karenina, Part 3, ch. viii.

Bird shooting

This description of a shoot entices Tolstoy, himself a keen sportsman, into one of his rare descriptions of outdoor scenery. The account of the shooting itself must be one of the most graphic accounts of a sport in all literature.

33

Grey old Laska, following close on his heels, sat down warily opposite him and pricked up her ears. The sun was setting behind the great forest and the birch trees dotted about in the aspen-grove stood out clearly in the evening glow with their drooping branches and their swollen buds ready to burst into leaf.

From the thicket, where the snow had not all melted, the water flowed almost noiselessly in narrow, winding streamlets. Tiny birds chirped and occasionally fluttered from tree to tree.

The intervals of profound silence were broken by the rustle of last year's leaves, stirred by the thawing earth and the grass growing.

'Why, one can hear and see the grass growing!' thought Levin, noticing a wet, slate-coloured aspen leaf moving beside a blade of young grass. He stood listening, and gazing down now at the wet, mossy ground, now at the watchful Laska, now at the sea of bare treetops that stretched on the slope below him, now at the darkening sky streaked with little white clouds. Slowly sweeping its wings, a hawk flew high over the distant forest; another followed unhurriedly in the same direction and vanished. In the thicket the birds chirped louder and more busily. Nearby a brown owl hooted, and Laska gave a start, took a few cautious steps, and, putting her head on one side, pricked up her ears again. A cuckoo was heard on the other side of the stream. It called twice on its usual note, and then gave a hoarse, hurried call and broke down.

'Fancy, the cuckoo already!' said Oblonsky, appearing from behind a bush.

'Yes, I can hear,' replied Levin, reluctantly disturbing the silence of the wood, his voice sounding disagreeable to himself. 'It won't be long now.'

Oblonsky's figure went behind the bush again and Levin saw nothing but the flare of a match, followed by the red glow of a cigarette and a spiral of blue smoke.

'Tchk! tchk!' came the clicking sound of Oblonsky cocking his gun.

'What's that cry?' he asked, drawing Levin's attention to a long-drawn whine like the high-pitched whinnying of a colt in play.

'Don't you know? It's a hare. But no more talking! Listen, they're coming!' Levin almost shouted, cocking his gun.

They heard a shrill whistle in the distance and, two seconds later—the interval the sportsman knows so well—another followed and then a third, and after the third whistle the sound of a hoarse cry.

Levin looked to right and left, and there, straight in front of him against the dusky blue sky, above the blurred tops of the tenderly sprouting aspen-trees, he saw a bird. It was flying straight towards him: the guttural cry, like the even tearing of some strong fabric, sounded close to his ear; the long beak and neck of the bird were already visible and, just as Levin was taking aim, there was a red flash from behind the bush where

107

Oblonsky was standing and the bird dropped like an arrow, then fluttered up again. Another flash, followed by the sound of a hit, and beating its wings as though trying to keep up in the air, the bird stopped, remained stationary for a moment and then fell with a heavy thud on the muddy ground.

'Did I miss it?' shouted Oblonsky, who could see nothing for smoke.

'Here it is!' said Levin, pointing to Laska, who, with one ear raised, wagging the tip of her shaggy tail, moving slowly as if to prolong the pleasure and almost smiling, was bringing the dead bird to her master. 'Well, I'm glad you got it,' said Levin, at the same time feeling envious that he had not shot the snipe himself.

'A wretched miss with the right barrel,' replied Oblonsky, loading his gun. 'Ssh . . . here's one coming.'

Indeed, they could hear a quick succession of shrill whistles. Two snipe, playing and chasing one another, and whistling but not crying, flew right above the sportsmen's heads. Four shots rang out and the snipe turned swiftly like swallows and vanished from sight.

Anna Karenina, Part 2, ch. xv.

In this book I have limited myself to taking excerpts from three novels and five of Tolstoy's many short stories. One glance at pages 110 to 111 of the Bibliography will show what a small proportion of his total output this represents. If it were possible to illustrate the range of his subject matter in a series of excerpts, they would have to include samples of his writings on religion and on education, extracts from his plays and his children's stories, specimens of his books and essays on ethics and aesthetics. But however long the selection went on it would still be inadequate. Tolstoy's achievement is too great for a cross-section to be taken of it.

But with Tolstoy, more than with most writers, it is important to know where to start reading him. I think that these eight works provide the best introduction and that anyone who reads them will want to read more.

Bibliography

Childhood, Boyhood and *Youth*
The Cossacks (containing also *The Death of Ivan Ilyich*
   and *Happy Ever After* (*Family Happiness*))
War and Peace
Anna Karenina
Resurrection
   All translated by Rosemary Edmonds in The Penguin
   Classics Series. Translations published respectively in
   1964, 1960, 1957, 1954, and 1966.

Signet Classics publish:

The Death of Ivan Ilyich and Other Stories (1960) (con-
   taining also *Family Happiness, Master and Man, The
   Kreutzer Sonata*)
   Translated by Aylmer Maude and J. D. Duff with an
   Afterword by David Magarschack
Anna Karenina
   Newly translated with an Introduction by David
   Magarschack
The Cossacks and *The Raid*
   Newly translated by Andrew MacAndrew
Resurrection (1961)
   Translated by Vera Traill

The World's Classics (Oxford University Press) publish:
   Childhood, Boyhood and Youth
   A Confession, and What I Believe
   What Then Must We Do?

What is Art? and Essays on Art
The Kingdom of God and Peace Essays
War and Peace
Anna Karenina
Resurrection
Twenty Three Tales
Tales of Army Life
The Kreutzer Sonata and Other Tales
Nine Stories
Recollections and Essays

Biographical works

MAUDE, AYLMER, *The Life of Tolstoy*, Oxford University Press, London 1930 (2 vols.).

TROYAT, HENRI, *Tolstoy*, W. H. Allen, London 1967. An excellent book which achieves almost a Tolstoyan richness of texture.

Critical works

(a) BOOKS

BAYLEY, JOHN, *Tolstoy and the Novel*, Chatto and Windus, London 1966. A valuable assessment of all the major works, seen against the Russian background.

BERLIN, ISAIAH, *The Hedgehog and the Fox*, Simon and Schuster, New York 1955. A useful and penetrating study of Tolstoy's view of history.

LAVRIN, JANKO, *Tolstoy. An Approach*, Methuen, London 1944. A provocative interpretation.

REDPATH, THEODORE, *Tolstoy*, Bowes and Bowes, London 1960. A sound introductory survey.

STEINER, GEORGE, *Tolstoy and Dostoyevsky*, Peregrine Books, London 1966. A detailed and stimulating comparison.

(b) ESSAYS AND ARTICLES

ARNOLD, MATTHEW, 'Count Leo Tolstoi', reprinted in *Essays in Criticism*, Second Series, Macmillan, London 1888. Interesting as representative of contemporary reactions to Tolstoy.

BIBLIOGRAPHY

DAVIE, DONALD, 'Tolstoy, Lermontov and Others', reprinted in Donald Davie (ed.), *Russian Literature and Modern English Fiction. A Collection of Critical Essays*, University of Chicago Press, 1965. Valuable on *The Kreutzer Sonata* and Tolstoy's relation to Pushkin.

GIFFORD, HENRY and WILLIAMS, RAYMOND, 'D. H. Lawrence and *Anna Karenina*', also reprinted in *Russian Literature and Modern English Fiction*. An exchange of letters about Lawrence's strictures on *Anna Karenina*.

LAWRENCE, D. H., 'Thomas Hardy, Verga and Tolstoy', from *The Study of Thomas Hardy in 'Phoenix'*, Heinemann, London; Viking Press, New York 1936. Lawrence at his silliest.

LEAVIS, DR. F. R., *Anna Karenina*, first published in the *Cambridge Quarterly*, Winter 1965-66, reprinted in *Anna Karenina and Other Essays*, Chatto and Windus, London 1967. An excellent assessment.

MEREZHKOVSKY, D. S. 'Dostoievsky and Tolstoy,' and 'Tolstoy as Artist', two essays both written in 1902 and both reprinted in *Russian Literature and Modern English Fiction*. Both short and both extremely perceptive; still among the best comment ever made on Tolstoy.

ORWELL, GEORGE, 'Lear, Tolstoy and the Fool', in *Shooting an Elephant and Other Essays*, Secker and Warburg, London 1950. On Tolstoy's attack on Shakespeare in a little-known pamphlet, *Shakespeare and the Drama* (1903).

RAHV, PHILIP, 'Concerning Tolstoy', an essay from the *Partisan Review* reprinted in *The New Partisan Reader*, Harcourt Brace, New York 1953. A good comprehensive assessment of Tolstoy's achievement.

TRILLING, LIONEL, *Anna Karenina*, an essay written as the introduction to the Limited Editions Club edition of the novel and reprinted in *The Opposing Self*, Secker and Warburg, London 1955. A brief and fairly slight but pleasant essay.

Tolstoy's works

* Dates are those of first publication in Russian.

TOLSTOY'S WORKS

1857 *Lucerne*

1859 *Three Deaths*

1859 *Family Happiness*

1860 *Polikushka*

1861 *Linen Mesurer* (History of a Horse)

1862 *Pedagogical Articles from Yasnaya Polyana*

1862 *The School at Yasnaya Polyana*

1863- *The Decembrists*
1878

1864- *War and Peace*
1869

1869- *Fables for Children*
1872

1869- *Natural Science Stories*
1872

1873- *Anna Karenina*
1876

1875 *On Popular Education*

1879- *A Confession*
1882

1881 *What Men Live By*

1881- *Critique of Dogmatic Theology*
1882

1881- *The Four Gospels Harmonised and Translated*
1882

1884 *What I Believe*

1884- *The Death of Ivan Ilyich* and other stories
1886

114

TOLSTOY'S WORKS